FINDING PEACE IN PAIN
Reflections of a Christian Psychotherapist

Yvonne C. Hebert, M.A., L.M.F.C.C.

LIVING FLAME PRESS
LOCUST VALLEY, N.Y. 11560

Cover: Robert Manning

All Bible references are from *The New American Bible,* 1971 edition.

Copyright: 1984: Yvonne C. Hebert, M.A., L.M.F.C.C.

ISBN: 0-914544-53-5

All rights reserved. This book or parts thereof must not be reproduced in any form without permission of the publisher.

Published by Living Flame Press/Box 74/ Locust Valley, N.Y. 11560

Printed in the United States of America

The afflicted and the needy seek water in vain,
Their tongues are parched with thirst.
I, the Lord, will answer them;
I, the God of Israel, will not forsake them.

I will open up rivers on the bare heights,
and fountains in the broad valleys;
I will turn the desert into a marshland,
and the dry ground into springs of water.
                                        Isaiah 41:17-18

Table of Contents

Preface	7
Introduction	13
One: Jesus Finds the Apostles Asleep	17
Two: Jesus Before Herod	23
Three: Mary's Passion	29
Four: The Fast of Jesus	35
Five: Jesus is Helped with His Cross	41
Six: The Crucifixion	51
Seven: Jesus Forgives	59
Eight: Jesus Again Before Pilate	73
Nine: The Betrayal	85
Ten: The Agony in the Garden	95
Eleven: The Way of the Cross	103

Even now I find my joy in the suffering I endure for you. In my own flesh I fill up what is lacking in the sufferings of Christ for the sake of His body, the church.

Colossians 1:24

Preface

As a Christian therapist, I am often moved by the spiritual and moral beauty of my clients—even while they are wrestling with difficult emotional distresses and problems of living.

Over the years I have come to two major conclusions about people. Many people seem afraid of their emotions and the emotions of others. I have at times wondered if I was observing something of a moral or social obligation not to show feelings, many times not even to our families. Sometimes, most especially *not* to our families.

While happy feelings are generally acceptable to others, painful emotions are so restricted in our society that many people have learned to be ashamed of feeling, let alone expressing, even to one other person, their feelings of pain, hardship and loneliness.

Yet we all have these emotions. In experiencing such feelings, we are more in need of support and concern from other human beings than at almost any other time in our lives. Yet it is in the throes of such feelings that we are usually the most isolated from human intimacy and compassion. If someone does perceive our pain, they can seldom find words to comfort us as we need. A rare touch of someone's hand, a hesitant expression of concern and encouragement is so often all that we receive for support in such times.

Watching this phenomenon in my own life and in the lives of others, I turned to God with the question, "Why?"

In my search for an answer, I encountered what I believe is a truth about every human being. I believe that every person experiences a sacred moment of the Passion in their own lives to share with Jesus.

What do I mean by this?

During each of our lives, I believe each of us experiences a painful emotion for which there is no relief. It may come to us only for a short period in our lifetime, or it may be a recurring theme throughout our lives.

No support from others, no expression of the feeling, can bring comfort or release. We must simply live with this pain until it leaves, whether by time or by a change in circumstances. I believe that if we carefully search the Passion of Jesus Christ, we will find a corresponding moment which Jesus suffered. By uniting our hurt with the pain of Christ, I believe we can share intimately in the Passion of Jesus and find strength and peace in our own suffering.

This can only be a gift from God, yet how seldom we see pain this way.

This book is a fictionalized account of the emotional suffering of a few friends and clients in my practice. These people moved into a spiritual union with Jesus by sharing His Passion as they experienced the pain in their own lives which they could not escape.

Some readers will feel the book is too emotional. I believe feelings are a gift from God—a way to know when we are being psychically damaged or called to emotional and spiritual growth. I embrace the release of emotive energy, whether happy or hurting, in an effort to recognize the meaning behind our emotions and to find healing. I hope that experiencing the reality of another's feelings will give my readers permission to feel and to talk of their own painful feelings without embarrassment, guilt or shame.

I am reminded of the statement attributed to St. Irenaeus. "The glory of God is a human being fully alive." Fully alive. Fully alive in body, mind and spirit. Fully alive to experience joy, intimacy and pain. Fully alive to share the beauty of our unique expression of life with God and other living things.

One of the criminals hanging in crucifixion blasphemed him: "Aren't you the Messiah? Then save yourself and us." But the other one rebuked him: "Have you no fear of God, seeing you are under the same sentence? We deserve it, after all. We are only paying the price for what we've done, but this man has done nothing wrong." He then said, "Jesus, remember me when you enter upon your reign." And Jesus replied, "I assure you: this day you will be with me in paradise."

Luke 23:39-43

Introduction

Positive emotional growth only flourishes in an atmosphere of love. But for many people raised in a climate of trauma and crisis, the meaning of love is distorted. With such a background, we may spend a lifetime searching for an unknown to fill a void in our lives which we can feel but cannot identify.

Our adult lives may reflect a frantic pattern of the same loveless traumas we abhorred as children. With study, we may come to understand love with our minds, yet our hearts may still be empty. How then can growth come into our lives?

To love we must first be loved. Somehow we must make that connection to someone who can help us experience a love satisfying to our needs. Since adults normally are uncomfortable with new feelings, taking part in such an exchange can be sufficiently painful that we find ourselves backing away from wholesome relationships, viewing them as threatening, and returning to the same dissatisfying milieu in which we were raised.

To move into love, then, can be a painful experience for us. It can mean changing the way we perceive life, God, other people and situations, even ourselves.

Part of this change involves our becoming aware of ourselves as loveable. To see ourselves as loveable, we must discard our feelings of being unworthy of love. To participate in a mutually satisfying love relationship, we must move through our fear of loving and being loved.

Somewhere, somehow, sometime in our lives this process of change must start if we are to mature emotionally as humans and spiritually as Christians.

Obviously, Christian psychotherapy can help us sort out our feelings and experiences and help us into a pattern which fosters emotional growth and healthy loving. For some people, it is an essential first step.

The various stages of prayer also can bring emotional healing into our lives if we aspire to a prayer of love.

The difficulty of moving into loving prayer for

a person who has feelings of fear and unworthiness cannot be over-emphasized. Such a person has no expectation of finding love in prayer, consequently does not seek it. Yet we live a life of death without love touching our spirits.

Taking the pain of our lives to the Lord in the sharing of His Passion opens us to the experience of Divine Love.

Sharing the Passion of Jesus is not easy. Pain is a part of the Passion, as it is a part of our lives. Sharing pain, even for a few seconds, is not pleasant.

Sharing the Passion of Jesus seems to require a brokenness of spirit where the person will come dumbly and with humility to Jesus, convinced that no hope exists for them in earthly solutions or human love. Such a person literally will be struggling for emotional survival and will be overwhelmed by pain.

Turning to the Holy Spirit we should pray for guidance in finding that precise moment with which we can most clearly identify. Prayerfully search the scriptural account of the Passion of Christ and let your heart search between the lines for your moment with Jesus.

Continue your prayer to the Holy Spirit. Ask Him to soften your heart to the Lord's love and wisdom. Desire to share your pain with the Lord and desire to share the pain of Jesus in His Passion. Meditate upon, or imagine yourself with Jesus, in your special moment of the Passion. Love Jesus in His pain. Let Him love you in your pain. Know that he is with you in your anguish.

There is a uniqueness about each of us before God that is so special I would not presume to suggest that there is only one way to meet the Lord in the sharing of His Passion. I only know that faithfully disposing yourself toward that sharing allows it to happen.

It should be noted that the same moments of the Passion may be viewed quite differently by each of us. For example, the Agony in the Garden can be perceived as a crisis of decision or as loneliness in conflict.

Loneliness can be found in many places in the Passion. Loneliness from inadequate human contact can be seen in the Agony in the Garden, Jesus finding the apostles asleep, in the denials of Peter, the betrayal of Judas, and Jesus meeting the weeping women. There are many other such places. Prayer gives us the wisdom to see exactly the moment that corresponds to our special need.

Spiritual loneliness is evident upon the Cross. "My God, my God, why have you forsaken me?"

Searching the Passion with prayer and faith can bring us to that exact moment, perhaps even that second, which we share with our Blessed Lord.

When we consider the physical suffering of Jesus throughout the Passion, I believe we will find corresponding similarities for physical pain.

This prayer has special significance for individuals in their growth in prayer. It appears that people sharing the Passion of Jesus find themselves in an experiential type of prayer that enables them to feel the love of God specifically directed to themselves.

Once we have experienced the love of God in a way uniquely satisfying to our soul, we have only to persevere through the various stages of contemplative prayer for emotional and spiritual growth to occur. There can be no turning back once we have learned to listen and to love with our hearts.

When we study the works of St. Theresa of Avila and St. John of the Cross, we see that for them contemplative prayer began after a time of great distress in which they experienced an unusual awareness of God's love for them.

Yet when we examine the lives of practicing Christians we see that few of them rise into contemplative prayer following periods of great emotional distress even though they are following the church's guidelines for holiness.

What causes this difference? With the mystics, as with the practicing Christian, a daily prayer life is functioning. Ascetic practices necessary for a dying to self and the world is also a part of the life of a practicing Christian and is certainly a part of the life of the great contemplatives. Following their unitive experiences with God, the saints returned to serve society with a joy and strength to maintain their own very special spiritual needs. Practicing Christians are also called to a life of service and social action. Times of crisis abound in the lives of Christians today as in the lives of the mystics of yesterday. What is the difference between the few who rise to unitive prayer and the many who stay embroiled in life's misery?

Perhaps the expectation of the individual is the only missing ingredient. If we are raised in a climate of emotional pain and fear, is it reasonable to assume that we will be free to anticipate great experiences of a loving God in our prayer life? If we are taught from childhood to feel unworthy of being loved or loving, how can we move into a prayer—or a life—of love?

Therapy may help people free themselves emotionally from feelings of unworthiness and could spark an unprecedented surge in contemplative prayer among the masses of Christians. If therapy were successful, such people would be able to believe in their heart that God is loving.

If people are even tentatively able to believe they could be loveable in the eyes of God, then the possibility of higher prayer exists. Then they can become aware that the painful experiences of life are not the anger of a raging God. Rather, a loving God is coaxing them to leave the troubles of the world behind and is calling them to a state of love in a higher consciousness.

The ingredients for contemplative prayer exist in every practicing Christian's lifestyle. The depths of such prayer would depend upon the individual's capacity to love.

The greatest challenge facing Christian therapists today could be to help people free themselves from their feelings of fear and unworthiness while encouraging them to see their current trauma as a springboard into the arms of God.

Perhaps the greatest challenge facing Christians today is the desire and the courage to change—releasing the feelings and patterns of the past and accepting a lifestyle of wholeness and healing love.

I

Jesus Finds the Apostles Asleep

In His anguish He prayed with all the greater intensity, and His sweat became like drops of blood falling to the ground. Then He rose from prayer and came to His disciples, only to find them asleep ...
                                    Luke 22:44-45

"I am just so scared." In the darkened room, with no ears to hear but my own, the words burst out in a torrent of pain. "Oh, God," I cried, "why is this happening to me? I am so afraid and I feel so alone."

On my knees, too frightened to cry, I prayed. I had prayed many times before, begging God for relief of my situation, but tonight was different. Tonight I felt broken. Twisted with such desperate, aching anxiety that my stomach felt raw. Chilled to the bone with a sense of isolation from other human beings. I felt my arms raise protectively over my own head and for a wild, hysterical moment I fought to keep from screaming.

My body was physically unable to sustain such racking emotion. This terrible fear and anxiety quieted a little, and I sat back, still shaking and cold. My mind numbed with panic.

When a coherent thought finally formed, it was brittle with rage. Rage at a God who sat so disdainfully distant.

"You're supposed to be a loving God. A just God. A merciful God. But you're a feelingless tyrant!" I raged. "Where is your mercy? How is this justice? Where is even a little compassion? You're supposed to be so powerful! How can you let such things happen to people? Don't you even listen a little?"

The uselessness of railing against such a deaf God crowded into my mind as a fresh wave of loneliness and fear tore at me.

"Why do I bother to pray?" I cried. "What would you know about this kind of pain, this kind of loneliness?"

"What do I know about such pain, such loneliness?" a voice spoke softly into my mind. "Perhaps a great deal. Perhaps if you would come with me to Gethsemani . . . Perhaps if you tried to share my sorrow . . . Perhaps you would find comfort for your own pain."

In the darkened room I sat quietly, barely breathing. Startled. Instantly peaceful. Was that the voice of Jesus? My mind churned with more thoughts than I could comprehend.

Deliberately, slowly, I made my way to a comfortable chair and sat down. Painstakingly I repeated the words I had heard. I listened to them spoken with my own voice, and I wondered about them.

All right. I would go to Gethsemani. I would try to share the sorrow of Jesus. I would try to understand what it would have been like to be Jesus that night. I would try to feel the pain and the loneliness of Jesus in the Garden the night before He was to die.

But where to start? Did I really know enough about the Passion of Jesus to attempt such imagining? Did I even know enough about Jesus? For a long moment I felt as though I might be trying something sacrilegious.

I turned on a light and pored over the account of the Passion in the Bible. It was so terse. Only the skeleton of the story. How could I know what He was thinking and feeling?

Reflectively, I glanced back through the stories of His public life, of His miracles and healings, of the times with the apostles. I tried to imagine myself there. How would I have felt knowing Jesus personally. Watching Him, listening to Him, eating with Him, doing all the homely, daily tasks which people must do to live.

The Agony in the Garden. Again, I had reached this place in the story of Jesus. I laid the Bible down and turned off the light and sat there.

"All right, Jesus, I am with you in Gethsemani.

Help me to share your agony. Help me to understand and feel just a little bit what it was like for you that night. Holy Spirit, soften my heart, enlighten my mind, that I may be open to my Lord."

The pictures flashed before my mind.

Jesus, in a candle-lit room, sharing food and conversation with his best friends.

Jesus, His heart growing heavy, walking into the moonlight and up the dusty road to Gethsemani followed by His cheerfully unaware friends.

Jesus, separating from all but three of His disciples, going deeper into the garden.

Jesus, telling these, His close friends, to pray, not for Him, but for themselves.

Jesus, alone now, moving through the trees in the darkness to a large, rough rock.

Jesus, the moonlight shining on His hair, kneeling in the grass and flowers of the Garden, His arms on the cold, gritty rock, His hands clasped.

How could I possibly imagine what He was thinking and feeling?

Laughing, taunting faces . . . hundreds of them.

A wooden post . . . chains . . . a cracking sound . . . a whip slashes through the air.

Peter, trusted friend, denying . . .

The hand of Jesus which had reached out with healing mercy to all who called on Him, drawn painfully over a piece of timber. A huge nail . . . an iron hammer . . . a burst of blood.

Jeering, angry faces . . . Jesus alone . . . jostling crowds, curious faces, indifferent faces, grieving faces . . . a narrow street between the buildings of the city . . . steps . . . pressing, shouting crowds, the rocks of the street rush upward as Jesus falls.

Jerusalem, city of stone, shining in the moonlight.

Jerusalem, torn and battered, in rubble.

Faces, all ages, all colors, changing, passing through centuries of time . . . frightened, laughing, grieved, sorrowing.

Jesus, gasping for breath, hanging nailed to the cross beneath an angry, boiling sky.

Taunting, upturned faces.

Faces, so many faces, crying out in despair, ignorant of the Good News of Jesus. Unaware of spiritual truths. Human faces . . . created for Heaven . . . so many would be lost because of the hardness of their own hearts.

The fury and pain and filth of hell.

The cunning, accusing, deceitful devil.

Faces, around the world, through centuries of time, hearing the Word, judging with standards of the material world. Hearing with deaf ears. Careless for their own spiritual safety.

A tangle of vines and thorns . . . a wreath of wooden spikes, a crown . . . descending . . .

Jesus, on the cross, being lifted up into the air, jolted and jerked, the weight of His body tearing His flesh and bones against the nails.

So many would never understand, or even care, what happened there that day.

Shouting, taunting, upturned faces.

Jesus, skin glistening with drops of sweat, rising from the rock, stumbling in the moonlight, hurrying back through the trees to His praying friends. They are all asleep.

I can feel the desolation.

"Join your pain with mine. Share my Passion with me," the voice said softly.

II

Jesus Before Herod

The chief priests and scribes were at hand to accuse Him vehemently. Herod and his guards then treated Him with contempt and insult, after which they put a magnificent robe on Him and sent Him back to Pilate.

Luke 23:10-11

She was a pretty woman, fiftyish, a little on the plump side, with a ready smile and a motherly warmth. She and her husband of 30 years gave the appearance of a truly devoted Christian couple. Most of their six children were already well into their own adult life situations.

"I guess you're wondering why I want marriage counseling," she said, nervously playing with her wedding rings. "We've been married for so long, you'd think we'd be used to each other by now."

"I know it's not always that simple," I smiled. "Feel free to say what's on your heart no matter how it sounds. We can work out the fine points later."

"I wish Ralph would have come too. I've never talked about him with anyone before," she said. "I feel like a traitor. But we were talking of a divorce a few years ago. Things were so bad. Marriage Encounter helped for a while. I know he's really trying. But," she bit her lip for a moment and then the words burst out, "it's just not enough. I'm so unhappy living with him!"

Her story wasn't that unusual. What was unusual was that these two people had clung together for 30 years in spite of the painful harshness of their relationship.

"I know he loves me as much as he's able," she cried. "He just doesn't trust me. He won't talk to me about anything that's real to him. He won't even discuss how he feels about anything. I have to guess all the time."

"What happens if you guess wrong?" I asked.

"Well, that's just it. Then he might not talk to me for days! Or he'll be real defensive and insult me, and I don't even know what I've done. His mother was like that too. She talked down to everybody. I hate it. I see our boys doing it . . . They even talk down to me! And to their sisters! And we won't have done anything to deserve it. They've just picked it up. I hate for them to be going into life talking to women like that!"

"How do you get what you need?"

"It's hard," she admitted bitterly. "I have to fight and tease and talk endlessly about what I want. No matter how little it costs. I feel so small sometimes. I feel like I have no worth at all. If Ralph wants something, he just buys it, but if I want something, well, I practically have to beg for it."

"Do you have your own spending money? Even a few dollars? Are you in a tight place financially?" I queried.

"Not anymore. We're really quite comfortable. It's not really the money. I could write a check, but then I have to explain why I wrote it and what each penny went for. Why, Ralph will go over every item on the grocery bill. What was this? Why did I buy that? What did we need this for? If he writes a check I don't do that to him!"

As Emily continued to come to therapy, she began to have a better understanding of her own behavior and that of her husband. She began to see that her husband's defensiveness grew out of his own fears and feelings of love deprivation and unworthiness.

With a clearer awareness of her husband's needs, she tried to be loving and supportive of him while at the same time developing assertiveness skills to help herself.

It was a difficult and emotionally draining experience for her. She said that she prayed for her husband and their marriage constantly. After he fell asleep at night, she would place her hand on him and pray that God would heal him emotionally so that he could learn to love and trust her.

"I'm trying to love him with the heart of Jesus," she said one afternoon. "But it's so hard. I was in the kitchen yesterday and he came out, shaking his finger at me, talking down and accusing me of something he thought I'd done—right in front of our son and his friends. It was just humiliating. He treated me like I was ugly and stupid—but even if I were, he shouldn't talk to me like that!" she mourned. "And then we had to get dressed up and meet another couple for dinner. I had to act like I loved him and was enjoying myself, but I felt such anger and bitterness toward him."

We were silent together for several minutes as she wept in rage and frustration. "I don't think I can take it much more," she said finally. "I'm really getting better at asserting myself for what I want. We've even agreed to a $10.00 a week allowance for each of us."

"Great!" I showed my hearty approval of these hard-won changes.

"But he's so mean sometimes. I just don't think I can go on much longer. He's never going to change."

The room was silent except for the sound of her weeping and the ticking of the clock.

"Lord, Jesus, now what?" I prayed silently. "What can I say to help her—to really help her? She's doing everything I'm telling her to do. She's trying so hard. In time, he'll change. They'll both change. But growth is so slow, and her life is so painful right now."

"Emily," I said slowly. "I want you to try something for yourself—something spiritual."

She waved her hands in a helpless, despairing gesture.

"I've come to believe that every human being experiences a certain moment in the Passion of

Jesus to share with Him. Perhaps being subjected to angry, accusatory outbursts, put-downs, insults and so on is that part of the Lord's Passion for you."

She looked at me, her forehead furrowed, a strange light in her eyes. "What am I supposed to do?"

"I don't know what you should do exactly. Just develop a way to share your pain with Jesus and accept some of His pain from that moment in His Passion with which you can most identify. Perhaps you can make up pictures in your mind or create an imaginary dialogue with Jesus—whatever seems to work for you. You'll think of a way unique to yourself, I'm sure."

"I'll try," she said. "God knows I've tried everything else. I don't want to leave him really."

****

"I don't know how to tell you how differently I feel since I talked to you last week." Emily sank into a chair and dropped her purse on the floor. "How can I tell you what this week has been like?"

I waited, silent.

She laughed suddenly. "Well, one thing is for sure. I really got to live the Passion of Jesus with Him. Ralph was a wild man all week."

"Live the Passion?"

"I didn't see how it could work. I really didn't. But I felt so comforted," she exclaimed. "I decided the part of the Passion I most identify with is when Jesus was on trial before Herod. Herod, the priests, the soldiers, all insulting and mocking Him. I tried to imagine the scene at first, but that didn't work for me. It seemed so distant.

"But then I got home, and right away Ralph accused me of something. I just placed my hand in the hand of Jesus and stood there with Him. Silent, as He was silent before His accusers. We faced Ralph and Herod together. I felt like I was really there with Jesus in Herod's Palace. But I wasn't. I was in my own living room. Only I wasn't alone. I really felt Jesus with me. I just told Him, in my heart, that I didn't want Him facing Herod and the others alone. Nor did I want to face Ralph alone. So I asked if we could live through those moments together and share the pain together. Jesus and I, we've been through those moments so many times this week." She paused. "It was painful, but I just felt peaceful through it. I stopped being afraid of Ralph. I think he knew it too."

"Who knew what?" I questioned. "I'm getting lost."

"Ralph," she answered quickly. "He seemed to know I was really changed. I think that's why he's been so upset all week. I'm so different. I'm asserting myself when I want something. I'm not getting hurt when he yells at me. I'm so different he's going to have to change—and soon. His ways are frustrating to him now!"

III

Mary's Passion

Near the cross of Jesus there stood His mother . . .
John 19:25

"I can't help her," he said. "She's my only daughter, she's dying, and I can't help her."

He leaned back in his chair and stared at me, his face rigid. "She's very angry at her sickness. I can't stand to see her die so angry and hurting. You've known us since before her mother died, so she might be comfortable with you. If you can help her come to some kind of peace . . . maybe that's too much to ask with so little time."

"I'll try," I said. "I'll do my very best."

"Of course," he left abruptly, a man beleaguered by tragedy. His wife had died suddenly three years before of stomach cancer. Now his daughter, only 20, had been diagnosed as being in advanced stages of the same disease. She had, at best, only a few weeks to live.

"I was so dumb. I saw the same doctor my mother did," she raged. "Why couldn't he have found it earlier? He has to be a quack! He killed my mother. He's killing me. And he's going to charge my father a fortune!"

She smashed her fist into the mattress and started to cry. "I don't want to die. My God, I don't want to die. I've only just started to live!"

I reached out to her, and she leaned against my shoulder, her frail body shaking.

"They try to keep me doped up all the time, but I won't let them. These are my last days on earth. I don't want to be unconscious through them! Why is this happening to me?"

Silently, I handed her some tissues.

"Can't anyone tell me? What did I do wrong? What did my mother do to get this cancer?"

"Betty," I stopped. Anything I could say seemed so futile.

She pulled away, clasped her arms around her abdomen and doubled over in pain.

"Betty, they're trying to help you be more comfortable. Maybe you should take some of the pain medications."

"I want to go home. Why can't I die at home? If I'm going to die anyway, why should anyone care where I do it?"

"They can give you better care here."

"I don't want their care. I needed them when I had a chance to live . . . But they couldn't find anything wrong with me then."

She laid back suddenly and covered her face

with her arm. "I'm being awful, aren't I? I don't want to be so angry acting, but I can't seem to help it."

"I understand, Betty. It's all right. It's better to get the anger out when you feel it."

"What possible difference can it make?" she said hopelessly.

"Betty, if you're going to die soon, there may be things you want to talk over with your father and with your friends. That's hard to do when you're feeling so much anger."

"I know. I just don't know how to stop feeling this way."

"It'll pass in time as you work on it."

"But I don't have time," she cried. "Oh, if only there were someone who could understand how I feel. If only there were a way to get past this anger fast, so I could talk to my dad. I know this is hurting him terribly."

"Betty," I hesitated. "Perhaps you could find peace if you thought about the Passion of Jesus . . . tried to share your pain with His pain . . ."

"What?" she shouted. "I'm 20 years old and I'm dying—and you want me to imagine how some weirdo felt dying 2,000 years ago!"

"Weirdo?"

"Yes. He was a weirdo. Going around saying the things He did. It's no wonder they killed Him."

"I thought you were a Christian."

"At least you've got the tense right! It's definitely 'were.' What kind of God would kill my mother and now me. I don't believe there is a God. I think the Bible is a joke."

"I don't believe that God killed your mother or that He is killing you," I said firmly. "But since that is what you believe right now, spiritual exercises such as I just suggested are definitely not for you.

Why don't you help me to understand how you're feeling. I do want to know. I do care that you're only 20, that you're in pain, that you've been told you're going to die soon. I do care, Betty."

She wept then, quietly, holding my hand.

* * * * *

As time passed, Betty became visibly weaker, but her anger and grief remained strong emotions. Gradually she gave in and accepted the pain medications.

The day came, as I knew it must, that her father met me at the elevator.

"She went into a coma last night," he said, walking down the hall with me. "The doctors don't expect her to come out of it."

We stood in the semi-darkened room and looked at the wisp of body beneath the sheets. Her face seemed to have aged beyond recognition. Her breathing was labored, her body jerking restlessly in spasms. Tears burned in my eyes.

"I'm truly sorry," I said. "She's a beautiful, spunky woman."

"I know." He walked back into the hallway, his hands fidgeting nervously in his pants pocket. "I want to thank you for helping her. We were able to have some good talks these last few days. You know that she went back to confession earlier this week."

"I'm glad of that."

"She was so angry with God. I was afraid to have her die like that." He looked at the ceiling and cleared his throat. "She shared with me what you said to her—about sharing her pain with Jesus. We both tried it."

"She didn't tell me."

"I think it helped her find peace. As a parent, watching my child suffer like that . . . Dear God, it's awful."

I nodded, feeling helpless to say anything of comfort to him, hoping that just being there, listening, would help.

"It must be terrible," I said finally to break the silence that seemed to throb between us.

"It is. It is. I tried sharing my feelings with Mary since she watched her son die. Tried to feel what she may have felt and thought. It helped some. I wouldn't have thought of doing that before. I would have prayed, of course, but sharing my feelings as a parent, joining my pain with hers, was different. It was hard to do, but it was worth it. I felt . . . supported."

He turned away, returning to stand near the bed of his daughter during her last hours on earth.

IV

The Fast of Jesus

He said to them: "I have greatly desired to eat this Passover with you before I suffer. I tell you, I will not eat again until it is fulfilled in the Kingdom of God."

Then taking a cup he offered a blessing in thanks and said: "Take this and divide it among you; I tell you, from now on I will not drink of the fruit of the vine until the coming of the reign of God."
Luke 22:15-18

"I've been trying to go on a spiritual fast for a day each week," Carol spoke slowly, carefully choosing her words. "I thought it might give me strength to diet the other six days."

"That sounds like a good idea," I nodded approvingly, "How is it working?"

"I'm not doing too well. I start feeling frantic

and, even though I try to pray, I'm defeated by early afternoon."

"Are you sure you're called to a spiritual fast?" I asked. "Maybe that's not what the Lord wants from you right now."

"It starts out feeling so right. And I did pray for guidance."

"I'm not entirely sure I believe in fasting for compulsive eaters." It was my turn to choose my words carefully. "Perhaps going on a starvation type fast will keep you flip-flopping from totally depriving yourself to bingeing and back to starving. Being on a dieting teeter-totter could trigger an emotional teeter-totter. Perhaps maintaining a steady, healthful diet every day could help to keep your emotions stable."

"It feels the other way around to me. I could stay on a diet if it weren't for my feelings. I get hurt so easily, I just think I'm going to die. I can't stand those feelings. They really tear me up," Carol leaned forward in her chair, straining to make me understand her. "I feel like I have to eat or I'll go mad."

"Do you really honestly think you'd actually die or go mad if you didn't eat when you have those hurt feelings?" I asked.

Carol looked at her hands considering my question carefully. "Yes," she said finally. "But not just when I'm hurt about something. Anything can set me off. If I'm bored or excited. If I'm afraid or happy, frustrated . . ." She took a deep breath and sighed. "Everything makes me feel, and my reaction is always to suppress the feeling.

I eat. It's like I don't know anything else that always works."

"But why do you need to suppress the feeling," I persisted. "What would happen to you if you just sat down and felt your feeling?"

"I think I'd explode. I might hurt someone. Do you know how many people I've offended because I tried to express myself and got carried away with too much emotion? My feelings aren't acceptable—to me or to anyone else. That's why I thought I needed spiritual fasting. It would teach me discipline."

"Fasting is biblical," I agreed. "Jesus fasted a lot."

"I could fast too, the way Jesus did it," Carol stated dryly. "He went off into the desert by himself. No kids, no relatives, no one demanding things of him, no one misunderstanding him or fighting with him. No daily demands or deadlines. He just walked away from it all."

"Has it occured to you that Jesus was fasting during His Passion?"

She looked at me, startled. "How do you know that?"

"Matthew, Mark and Luke all say so," I said. "Jesus was fasting during His trial, during the scourging, when He carried the cross, when He was nailed to the cross. Jesus spent the most difficult day of His life fasting."

"Dear God," Carol murmured, "how awful that must have been,"

"Awful to the natural body," I mused thoughtfully. "But I think Jesus used fasting as a way to gain spiritual and inner strength. Perhaps you could join the panic and pain felt in your life with the pain Jesus felt during His Passion. Perhaps you would find the strength to change your eating habits, if, in times of trial, you joined your emotional pain with that of Jesus, with the intention of sharing the pain of Jesus' Passion with Him."

"How am I supposed to do that?" Carol queried, her eyes serious.

"Pray for guidance and grace first, I think. Then have an imaginary conversation with Jesus about things He might have felt or thought, or meditate on various scenes of the Passion as you think it might have been. Whatever will help you feel close to the sufferings of Jesus."

"I'll try," she said shortly, "but I'm upset all the time. I'd never get anything else done."

* * * * *

Carol did not bring the subject up again for two weeks. "I lost a little weight this week," she confided shyly.

"How great," I applauded. "What did you do?"

"Didn't eat."

We both laughed.

"I tried that meditating you suggested. It didn't seem to work for me."

"It didn't?" I said, surprised.

"Well, I don't know," she was quiet a moment. "It did and it didn't. It's hard to explain. I tried. When it was getting close to quitting time, I tried to imagine being with Jesus in the courtyard with the soldiers waiting for morning. I tried to imagine being cold and thirsty with everyone talking mean. When I had responsibilities that were getting to be too much, I tried to think of Jesus carrying the cross weak from hunger. Or speaking his feelings out from the cross with all those people listening. I don't know how He did that."

"And you felt no strength from trying to share this with Jesus?" I questioned her.

"I can't say that I did. I felt a deeper understanding of the Passion. As a Christian I'm grateful for that, but I can't say that I felt anything while I was trying to."

"You didn't feel anything while you were trying to," I repeated. "What do you mean? Did you feel something later?"

"Nothing for a few days. It was sort of gradual . . . I still don't feel anything when I think about the Passion. But what's strange is that I've developed a real compassion for other fat people. I've never liked other fat people. I've avoided them. Almost hated them. Thought they were lazy and sloppy. I didn't want to be like them."

"How interesting," I said, trying not to think of my own generous proportions.

"But after a few days I found myself feeling peaceful towards them. More than peaceful—compassionate. A few days ago I found myself praying for a fat woman I saw who was really uncomfortable. I found myself asking Jesus to help her. I tried then to share my distress over my compulsive eating with His Passion and asked the Lord to give her the benefits of my prayer. Then I felt good."

"Now that's really interesting," I mused out loud. "Are you continuing to do that?"

"Every time I see a fat person." She laughed suddenly. "I eat out a lot, because I work. It does seem that the Lord is sending a fat person within my line of vision every time I sit down to eat. It's getting hard to overeat when I'm praying for someone else who's eating too much."

V

Jesus is Helped with His Cross

As they led Him away, they laid hold of one Simon the Cyrenean who was coming in from the fields. They put a crossbeam on Simon's shoulder for him to carry along behind Jesus.

Luke 23:26

The sun was warm on my hair, but the air was still cool. I sat back in the lounge chair truly savoring the morning freshness in this quiet, mountain retreat. Birds sang inquisitively as they busied themselves with their spring chores. My vacation. One week spent with other Christians for a spiritual retreat. A time for silence and sharing, for mutual support and healing.

As I watched some of these people moving

about the retreat grounds, my attention was drawn to a young man walking purposefully toward me across the lawn. We had met a few days earlier when we had been assigned to similar housekeeping chores for the week. As the days slipped by, I had noticed that in spite of the prayers, music and spiritual messages from the retreat master, I was feeling a continuing heaviness from John.

"You really seem unhappy," I had said to him the evening before. "Is there anything I can do to help?"

His brown eyes somber, he had regarded me quietly for a moment. "I am unhappy," he said. "But I don't think there's anything you can do to help. I've talked with doctors, psychiatrists, psychologists and ministers. I have to live with a certain burden, and I don't want to."

"I'm sorry it's so heavy for you. Would you like to talk about it?"

"Not really, but I will. Although I don't expect to find an answer any more. I'm just sorry it's coloring my personality so much that another person can tell by looking at me that my spirit is in pain."

"John," I chided him gently, "I'm not just another person. I'm trained to see emotional pain. I'm sure most people wouldn't notice. Besides, perhaps the Lord has given me a special sensitivity to you. That is why we're here."

"Right," he allowed a smile to touch his lips, "but we're a little short on time now. How about after breakfast tomorrow?"

I smiled up at him when he approached the next morning. "It's going to be a gorgeous day, John."

"Yes," he nodded and sat down. His shoulders bent forward as he rested his chin on his cupped hands. His eyes studied me unwaveringly. Accustomed to giving orders and being obeyed without question, accustomed to searching for answers in science and in the training and expertise of humans, he was following the pattern of his life in keeping his appointment with me, however futile the effort appeared to be. I prayed silently that the Lord would speak through me to heal him of his burden, or the bitterness he felt toward his burden.

"Well," he said finally, "it's my arm. I know you've seen I have a weak right arm."

"You do?" I exclaimed. "I mean, no, I hadn't noticed. What's wrong?" Impulsively I leaned over and looked at his forearms, first one, then the other. The right arm was smaller. His shirt sleeves were short but covered the arm above the elbow. I reached over and raised the sleeve. The upper arm was barely larger than the forearm.

"Why?"

"Polio. When I was a kid."

"Oh."

"It doesn't straighten all the way out, either. It's just weak. Too weak to do things other people take for granted, like opening a catsup bottle.

"I see."

"People have to do things for me. I steady the stool while my wife changes the lightbulbs. I can't screw them in tight enough, or unscrew them at all. I hate it. She says she doesn't mind. But I feel like half a man. Sometimes people have to help me, and they don't want to. I can see it in their

43

eyes. They're stuck, and they have to help me. I don't want to ask them, but I have to. I feel degraded."

"That would be hard to live with."

"It is. I can do some things with my arm. I can steady things. I can pick things up sometimes, but all at once there will be no strength left. Sometimes I can't do simple things I could do the day before. I never know when it's not going to work right."

We sat quietly for a few minutes with his story resting between us. He played with a leaf from a nearby bush, turning it idly between his fingers.

"There's more?" I finally questioned.

With a sigh he threw the twig away and leaned back. He told me of the pain of his family's search for a doctor who could cure him when he contracted polio. He spoke of his fears when he lay in bed for months as a boy semi-paralyzed, and his guilt at being unhappy with his current situation when he could walk again and use his arm for many things. After all, the worst had not happened to him. He could have been permanently paralyzed. But he wanted to be perfect, to be like other people.

He had spent a fortune on psychotherapy trying to reconcile his emotions to his condition, but it had only been partially successful. He had talked with ministers about his guilt and his anger at his situation, but again the resolution of his conflicts had been incomplete. In spite of his desire to be happy, his spirit was sad and the wound in his soul was torn again every time his arm proved inadequate to the task of living like a man.

"John," I reached my hand out to him, searching for words. He looked at me with an intense calmness, his eyes unable to mask the defeated resignation he felt about his life. His attitude was expectant and curious, but I recognized that he knew there was no human solution. His curiosity was detached, impersonal. He was abstractedly observing how I would tell him that I could not help him make a better adjustment to his life than he already had.

"On a human level, I guess it's just something you have to live with."

"Yes," he said, amusement touching his lips at my abruptness.

"But on a spiritual level, I'm sure there is healing possible."

"I've prayed. Do you think I haven't prayed?" Impatiently he drew back from me. "My God, how I've prayed—for strength, for healing, for understanding. Of course it's helped, but I'm still a cripple and," he added with emphasis, "still *feel* like a cripple."

"I was thinking more of a sharing prayer."

He stared at me, his eyes offended, leaning back in his chair, one foot across the other leg's knee. He had separated himself from me as fully as he could without walking away.

"I've prayed with other people too," he said flatly.

"John, I've found another way to pray," I said quietly. "I've come into a new understanding of life and the difficulties of life, and it's given me a new way of praying."

He didn't speak or move, so I went on.

"I've begun to believe that each of us has a moment of His Sacred Passion to share with the Lord, as quickly or as fully as we wish to share it. I'm finding that when we share Jesus' Passion with Him, our pain takes on meaning and becomes a blessing."

"I don't understand what you're saying. Jesus did not have a crippled arm."

My mind raced frantically through the story of the Passion, looking for just that second that John could share with Jesus. "But He did, John," I burst out. "He did. It was His Passion, His gift to God for our sins, His cross to bear . . . but He could not. He became too weak. He had to have help."

"He fell three times."

"More than that, the cross was finally taken from Him and given to Simon of Cyrene . . ."

"Who didn't want it. He didn't want to help with the cross. They had to make him carry it for Jesus." John inserted, his eyes snapping.

"His arm was just too weak to carry his cross any further. John, can you see that you share that moment with the Lord? Lying face down in the dirt, beaten and weak but with a job to do and the desire to do it, but His body is too weak to go any further. His arm just won't circle that cross again. He can't grasp it with enough strength to hold onto it."

"I've never related to that before, but I can kind of see the similarity. So what do I do?"

"I don't know what you'll do. I know that I meditate successfully on my moment of the Passion. Other people I've talked with do other things. One woman says she can imagine herself right there with Jesus and lives the moment in her own life, sort of. Other people share their feelings, they talk to God, or pray, or try to imagine what Jesus was feeling. It seems that everyone winds up sharing their moment with the Lord in His Passion a little differently. Each of us is so unique, I guess once we recognize our moment of suffering as something very special, very intimate with Jesus, a kind of union with Him, something that no one but us shares with Him, we find a very special way of sharing that moment with Jesus."

"I'm a little uncomfortable with it. Can we try to do it together once. Can we pray it somehow?"

"Of course." I reached out for his hands, and we sat with heads bowed together, hands clasped, the sun warm on our backs. We sat silently for a moment and let the sounds of the world around us touch us: the laughing and talking of passing people—the birds singing to the world—the rustle of wind and small creatures in the grass and leaves.

"Dear Lord," I prayed. "I know this almost useless, crippled arm can be John's moment of the Passion to share with You. Help us find the words, the thoughts, the way of sharing that will best bring John into an understanding of that moment when you, too, could not do the work with your arm that you had to do.

"When you lay, bleeding and exhausted, in that dusty road with the cross cutting into your back, leaning heavily against your head, pressing the thorns deeper into your head and neck, gouging your flesh . . .

"May we feel, may we share, the very human panic that you must have felt, the confusion, the terror and pain of that moment.

"You fall and cannot get up again. You try to move, but your body will not, cannot, move. It cries out in physical agony and exhaustion.

"And yet, you must reach Calvary. The soldiers are shouting, and pulling on the ropes around your body, dragging you against the cross. You try to raise yourself, to place your hand on the ground, to push yourself up, but it fails. It buckles under your weight, and you drop again to the dust.

"It is your destiny, your cross to bear, the work you have come to do. You must get up, somehow you must get up. Somehow you must lift that cross again. But your arms are like rubber . . .

"But what has happened? The cross is being lifted away from you, and you gasp for the sudden breath of air that you are able to take with the weight gone from your chest.

"You are being dragged to your feet with rough, bruising hands. The thorns tear your flesh as you are pushed to your feet, your head reels from loss of blood and the endless pain.

"And then you see his eyes. His angry, sullen eyes. He is staring at you with undisguised resentment, and you recognize that he is holding your cross on his own shoulders.

"He does not want to. He does not want to help you with your cross. He does not wish to be involved with you. Or to spend his time this way.

"He is being forced to help you with your burden, and his resentfulness cuts through you like a dagger. Another kind of scourging, being helped by someone who does not wish to help.

"Your parched lips try to speak, to thank him, to touch his heart so that he will want to help, but he turns with disdain, and without looking at you again, easily and skillfully carries your cross behind you.

"It is so easy for him, so impossible for you. Your arms are trembling with weariness, your body, your entire physical system is in shock from the brutality of the scourging and the pain, the stinging, blinding, aching pain . . .

"Oh, God, let us share that moment with you as much as we can, know in that moment as you face his eyes, his angry eyes, that we, too, are being helped by someone who does not want to help us, who must help us because we are too weak, because our arm will not do what it was made to do, what everyone else seems able to do . . .

"Lord, let us share your pain. Share our pain, be with us, let us be with you. Know that we care that there was no one there who wanted to share your cross . . ."

His grief stopped my prayer. The tears were falling without shame across our hands. We prayed silently then, each of us in our own thoughts, our own unique experience of the Lord.

"I'm not sure," he said later as we were walking slowly across the lawn, "when you do this kind of prayer. Do you set aside a time to meditate, or when you're hurting, or every day as you feel like it?"

"I have the most success with this kind of prayer when I'm into the hurt, John. When I'm feeling the pain of my life. When my cross is suddenly evident, and I'm feeling it, seems the best time to share it with the Lord, even for just a few seconds."

We stopped at the entrance to one of the buildings.

"I have to leave you here," he said. "I just don't know about all this. I have to go somewhere and think about it."

I watched him walk away and noted that the heaviness was still with him. My prayer had touched me, but it hadn't been entirely right for him, I knew.

A few hours later as I sat in the dining room with friends, John entered, and my heart skipped with gladness. He was touched with joy. He saw me and came over immediately.

"I found my way to share," he said, his eyes sparkling with energy and openness. "You're right. It works. I'm happy. I'll never be the same again."

VI

The Crucifixion

Two insurgents were crucified along with him, one at his right and one at his left. People going by kept insulting him, tossing their heads and saying: "So you are the one who was going to destroy the temple and rebuild it in three days! Save yourself, why don't you? Come down off that cross if you are God's son!" The chief priests, the scribes, and the elders also joined in the jeering: "He saved others but he cannot save himself! So he is the king of Israel! Let's see him come down from that cross and then we will believe in him. He relied on God; let God rescue him now if he wants to. After all, he claimed, 'I am God's son!'" The insurgents who had been crucified with him kept taunting him in the same way.

Matthew 27:38-44

"She's gone," he sat down, still shaken from the

morning's events. "We were supposed to start our vacation this morning. She came in the bedroom and woke me up at 5:30 A.M. She'd already loaded her car up with her clothes. She said she couldn't stand going away with me—being alone with just me and the kids all day every day for two weeks. She said she needed a rest. She said she didn't know when she'd be back."

He sucked in his breath and leaned back, staring at the ceiling.

"I knew she was going. I told you a month ago she was going. I told you she wasn't going on vacation with me. I knew it, I felt it coming. My God, I don't know what to do!"

"The kids?" I questioned.

"Left them with me. All five. Cancelled the baby sitter for two weeks. Took all the cash and travelers checks we had for the trip. She said she needed it for her trip. I don't even know where I'll get the money to feed those kids." He pounded his fist on the couch beside him in utter frustration.

"She hates me. She has to. How could she do this if she didn't hate me?"

"Do you think she hates the kids too?" I asked.

"How could she do this to her kids? I couldn't leave those little fellas. Where is her mother's instinct? They've been crying all day, calling for her. It's driving me crazy. When I left to come over here, they were hanging on my legs, scared to death I was leaving too."

"Your children are so young, Al. Only one of them is over six. How do they know this is so serious?"

"Because we were all leaving this morning. They're young, but they know we were all going somewhere. The three older ones have been camping before. They were really excited about the trip. They woke up with their mother packing the car. We had a big scene, and she left. The kids and I just sat there staring at each other." His body stretched compulsively, explosively, as if he were about to break through his own skin. "She hugged and kissed each of them goodbye and told them she'd call them in a few days from wherever she went. She apologized to them for leaving them with me! She said she'd send for them when she could. She did everything she could to upset them before she left! My God, I don't know what to do!"

"I know I've done wrong. I wasn't a good husband the first few years of our marriage. But I've changed. I have changed. You know I have!"

"Yes, I know you have, Al. You really are a different man than you were."

"She never left me when I was drinking. No matter how bad I got, she stuck right there and tried to change me. Now I'm doing what she wants and she leaves. Why didn't she leave when I was making life miserable for her?"

We sat quietly for a moment. Al, covering his face with his hand, wept quietly.

I remembered back to our first meeting. His wife, Betty, had come to see me. She loved her husband, she said, but he drank and had a fierce, rebellious temper. He was abusive to their children, and she did not wish to have any more children by him. She didn't know how she could continue to live with him if he didn't become more domesticated. To the amazement of both of us, Al not only came to therapy when she asked him to, he returned to church shortly thereafter. A few weeks later, in the early morning hours she had woken. He was missing from the bedroom. Betty found him in the living room, on his knees, weeping. He had had an experience of God that had touched him profoundly. He was a new man, he said. She cautiously tried to believe him.

He had changed. There were only rare occasions when he had a drink. Al became the head of his family with a fervor that was as upsetting to Betty as his previous behavior had been.

"I love her," he burst out, bringing me back to the present. "I don't want to live without her. I feel married to her. I feel we're married before God. That we're one person. I was married twice before Betty. I had kids with one of my first wives. But I never felt married before Betty. When I stood at that altar, I knew it was right. I knew I finally had a real wife. I don't want to lose her. I know I've done wrong, but I've changed, and I'll keep on changing as much as I need to, to keep her."

*****

During the next few weeks, I met with Al several times. He needed help to release the distressing emotions he was feeling and to sort out practical solutions for the problems with which he was being confronted.

During these sessions, it became clear that relationships with loved ones had been fraught with emotional and physical peril since he was a baby. He had physically been beaten by his father so often and so hard that he had feared he would not always live through the beatings.

When he was a preteen he had been caught in a sexual exploration with a neighbor girl some years older than himself by his two younger sisters. Unaware of the grievous emotional damage they were causing, they had threatened to tell their father on Al for years thus forcing him to do things for them that he did not wish to do. He had lived in terror, knowing the crippling beatings he had, and was, receiving for upsetting his father in everyday living. He had been certain that his father would surely destroy him for such a serious offense. At 15, he fled his home and did not return until his father had died.

His life had been a series of emotional tragedies. He had responded by living a life of anger, violence, drugs and alcohol. He had fought many men for the sheer pleasure he experienced hitting them.

Al had changed. There was no question of it. The drugs and alcohol and fighting were gone from him. He had learned new ways to discipline his children so that he was not an abusive father himself. He was, however, still an intense, emotionally guarded individual. He had much to learn about living in a family. His efforts to be a good husband and father, while well-intentioned, were still short of ideal in Betty's eyes. She reached a place where she wouldn't wait any longer.

At one of our sessions, Al described his

loneliness, fears and almost hysterical feelings of love deprivation to me. He was clearly forming new behaviors. His understanding of himself was growing well. But his despair at losing his wife was overwhelming him. At the end of our session, as we prayed, I suggested to him that he look for that moment of Christ's Passion with which he could identify. He listened gravely, asked a few tense questions, and listlessly agreed to try it. He left my office heavy with pain.

*****

"That's a powerful way you taught me to pray," he said a few days later as he took a chair in my office.

"What happened," I asked expectantly.

"I had a hard time getting into it," he admitted. "I thought about the Passion of Christ for quite a while. Lots of places I could identify with the Lord's suffering, but they didn't seem to touch me particularly. I finally fell asleep without any real feeling of prayer. I woke up a few hours later really hurting for Betty. Really missing her. It seemed like such rejection. I started remembering other times in my life when I had trouble with people. Then I realized I was lying in bed with my arms stretched out and my hands lying flat and open. My feet were crossed. I was in the position of Jesus on the cross, and I could really feel like I was being crucified too. So I started praying and identifying with Jesus crucified for sins He didn't commit. Crucified for my sins. It came to me after a while that I really don't think anyone in my entire life has ever forgiven me for anything I've ever done wrong."

"No one?" I queried.

"I don't think so," he said seriously. "I've tried to think of someone, and I can't. When I do wrong, people really pay me back. They punish me, and they don't stop. Look at my father . . . my sisters . . . and it's what Betty is doing now. She hasn't forgiven me for those first years. She's not forgiving me either for the mistakes I'm still making . . . and she's letting me know she's not forgiving me even though she knows I'm trying."

"What about you, Al? Are you forgiving yourself?"

His fist clenched compulsively, and he slammed it down on the arm of his chair. "Least of all," he said bitterly. "I forgive myself the least of anybody. Every wrong I've ever done is on my mind all the time. I can't forget, and neither can anyone else."

"The Lord really revealed a heavy area for you to work on," I observed. "Your lack of forgiveness for yourself is what makes you see unforgiveness from others. If you could let go of the past, other people could let go of the past also. But the Lord has forgiven you, and he has brought forgiveness to you . . . that's what the crucifixion is all about. He has forgiven you, and what the Lord forgives, He forgets."

"I can't quite grasp that," he leaned over and stared at the floor, his hands clasped in front of him, lips tight. "I'm trying, but I can't figure out what you're saying. I understand the words but they don't seem to have any meaning to me."

"I'm sure the Lord's forgiveness will have meaning for you if you continue to unite yourself with Jesus in His Passion. We can work on this feeling of being unforgiven here in therapy, and that will help at an emotional level."

He nodded. "I'll stay with it," he said quietly. "I sure don't have any place else to go. I really did feel the presence of Jesus when I identified with His crucifixion this morning. I felt strengthened. Understood. . . . Like my life had some meaning after all and in spite of it all. I didn't feel so alone being able to share my guilt for my sins with Jesus while He was suffering for them. I felt loved, I think, really loved, for the first time in my life."

VII

Jesus Forgives

Two others who were criminals were led along with him to be crucified. When they came to Skull Place, as it was called, they crucified him there and the criminals as well, one on his right and the other on his left. Jesus said, "Father, forgive them; they do not know what they are doing."

Luke 23:32-34

"Nobody loves me," she stated emphatically, "and no one ever has loved me. Most people don't even like me."

"That's a pretty heavy statement," I cautioned.

"Because it's heavy doesn't make it not true," she flashed back, her brown eyes snapping with anger.

"You're right, of course," I agreed quickly. "But your statement is generalizing across your family, friends, relatives, business acquaintances, neighbors . . ." my hand gestured sweepingly across a wide arc. "even time . . . perhaps 40 years . . . can you really say that *no one* has *ever* loved you?"

She was silent for a long minute. Her face set in an expression that was curiously both hard and hurt. It was the first time I had met her, and she had seemed so gentle as to be defenseless when she had entered my office. I was delighted to see that she was able to express her feelings of anger.

"I think a few people have wanted to love me . . . or like me . . . but not when they get to know me."

"It's something you're doing then, that alienates people?"

"Yes."

"Do you know what you're doing?"

"More what I'm not doing. I can't talk."

I raised an eyebrow and leaned back in my chair looking at her intently. "You seem able to talk just fine."

"But I can't really. I freeze. I just don't have anything to say. Thoughts go in and out of my mind so fast I can't catch any of them—or I can't think of anything at all. I'm a social retard. And it hurts."

She was silent again, folding and unfolding the leather strap of her purse. "I've tried everything I can think of . . . conversation courses, assertiveness training, charm school, dancing class, group therapy, social clubs . . . the list is endless. I still can't talk. I still don't have anyone that wants to be with me as much as I want to be with them."

"But you've been very successful in business. You couldn't have done that without talking. You're obviously liked and respected on your job."

"Yes, but business is structured. I know what to do, what's expected of me. There are mutual things to talk about, things that have to be talked about. I don't have to think of a topic. It's just there, and everyone knows what it is."

"Social situations are the primary trouble area."

"Yes."

"What about family situations? That should be semi-structured. There's a certain protocol within each family. Various behaviors that are agreed upon and ongoing activities."

"My family doesn't like me. Never has."

"Not even a little?" I pressed.

"Not even a little. I just don't fit into my family." Her face grimaced with pain and frustration. "I couldn't stand being left out all the time. I left home 20 years ago. I go back every couple of years, although I don't really know why. To fool myself I guess. Some of the family is OK. One of my sisters is polite. She's really a nice person. She tries to be nice to me. She doesn't know what to talk to me about. She'll sit there and give me the time if I can think of something to say."

"Does she have trouble talking to other people?"

"Doesn't seem to. She's married, four kids, Brownie leader, PTA, works part time. She seems to be OK."

"How was it when you were kids?"

She laughed ruefully. "No different. Everyone had something going on. I got lost in the shuffle. I couldn't seem to get anyone's attention. The whole family—five of us kids—could talk but me. Did I say talk?—No, they shouted. I couldn't shout. Nothing I did was important enough to get anyone to stop their life long enough to look at mine."

"I'm hearing a real anger from you, Sylvia."

"I am angry," she exploded. "What did I ever do to anybody? Why can't anyone notice me? Do I have to be hard and mean to get attention? Do I have to laugh loud and talk incessantly—people like that drain me! I don't see how other people stand them, but other people like people like that! She stopped abruptly and covered her face with her hand. "I feel tired just talking about it."

Her face tense, she leaned forward in her chair, one arm tight across her stomach. For a long moment I waited, wondering if she was going to be sick. Gently, then, her body began to rock ever so slightly forward and back as the tears began to flow.

"Can you tell me *why* when I've had a miserable, lonesome childhood, I have to have a miserable, lonesome adulthood? Can you tell me why? I don't think I can stand much more of this."

As we talked that afternoon and for several weeks thereafter a picture began to emerge of Sylvia. An unusually talented artist, she was characterized by a gentleness of soul that I rarely had experienced in a person. She had a reverence for life—any life, human or animal—

that appeared to have been born out of a childhood of incredible personal rejection and physical deprivation.

The family had been poor, poverty-stricken. Five children were left fatherless while all were still in grade school. Without a trade or skill, the mother had worked at the most menial jobs to keep the family together. It had been very hard for the mother and a very difficult childhood for the children. Somehow the other children had gone their ways, marrying and raising families within a few miles of each other. They appeared to have been toughened by their childhood experiences.

But Sylvia had not survived well. The family had treated each other with an indifferent casualness. Sylvia had needed much more and had interpreted her family's behavior as rejection.

Her life after childhood had a pathetic hollowness to it. Except for her business life, her personal life had been a succession of years of loneliness followed by a series of brief, frantic attempts at a love life with poorly chosen males and a retreat back into a confused loneliness. In spite of her professional and financial successes, she valued herself very little.

"It's as if I can't value myself until I see that someone else values me, and no one else ever does," she wept bitterly one afternoon. "I'd do anything for someone if they'd only love me—but that hasn't worked either. It seems the more you do for people, the less they value you."

"I don't think that's necessarily true," I interjected. "But there is a pattern to making friends.

Perhaps you do too much too soon. The other person might feel indebted and might back away from you because they felt uncomfortable—not because they didn't like you personally."

"I guess that's possible," she agreed listlessly.

"Go a little slower. Do a favor if it comes up . . . but wait for the other person to find a way to meet a need of yours before you do another favor."

"Tit for tat. How ugly!"

"But necessary. It allows a mutual friendship to blossom. Not a relationship based on dependence and/or bribery."

"I feel so anxious to have someone to do things with and for. I really want to care for someone."

"That may be part of why you can't talk, Sylvia. You're trying so hard to please the other person, you're not being yourself. Share your thoughts a little even if they don't please everyone. Try a little with ten people, and if one person is ready for your friendship, they'll respond. Then you'll have started a healthy relationship."

"It sounds so slow. I feel so lonely now."

"Your way is slower, Sylvia. The only people you'll find are people who will take until you're drained and then leave. You've been through that too often already."

"I know," she nodded her head, her lips drawn tight, "and that hurts."

As the weeks went by, Sylvia struggled to gain confidence in herself and to learn how to move into a successful friendship. She was proud of the progress she found herself making, but her inability to relate to her own family continued to distress her.

One day her usual poise was shattered. Flushed with anger, she arrived for her appointment and slammed into a chair. She tried to talk, but her emotions were so tumultuous she burst into tears instead.

I waited.

"I hate my family!" burst from her finally.

"What has happened?" I asked quietly.

"My mother called this morning. She's visiting my sister."

"Oh?"

"You wouldn't believe our conversation. No one would!"

"What did she say?"

Sylvia laughed suddenly, harshly. "She said it was a nice party. Everyone was there."

"What party?"

"That's what I asked her. She said the party at my sister's last Saturday. Everyone was there. She said there must have been 300 people there. *Everyone* was there.

"So I said, 'Gee Ma, that's a lot of people. What kind of party was it?' And she said, 'Why the family reunion. It was just marvelous! Everyone was there. All the women brought their favorite homemade dishes, all the little kids, so many little kids. Everyone was there!'

"And I said, 'Ma, whose family's reunion?' I thought maybe it was a brother or sister-in-law's family. But it wasn't. It was *my* family! Do you know what she said?" Sylvia stared at me, her eyes huge and dark with pain.

"She said, 'Why Sylvia, the Carsons', of course. And everyone was there! It was so exciting.' She went on telling me about it and every little while she'd say 'and everyone was there.'"

The tears were rolling down Sylvia's cheeks again. "Do you know what I did? Do you know what I did?"

"No," I responded quietly. "What did you do, Sylvia?"

"I stopped her. I said, 'Wait a minute, Ma. Wait a minute. I have something to say. Ma, I'm glad you had a good time at the party, but I wish you'd stop saying everyone was there. Everyone wasn't there. *I* wasn't there. I didn't even know about it'"

"Praise God!" I whooped. "Sylvia, that's great."

Sylvia smiled wanly, the tears still streaming. "She said she had told me. She said I probably wasn't listening when she told me. So I said OK, maybe I was told, and I didn't hear. I still didn't think she should say everyone was there. Then I told her someone should have written and invited me to be sure I knew about it."

"I am proud of you," I said emphatically. "It took a great deal of self-acknowledgement to say that. You took a risk with your family to be noticed and recognized as a person. I am pleased with what you did for yourself."

"I feel good in a way, but I feel awful, too."

"I'm not sure I understand."

"I'm glad I said something," she bit her lower lip for a minute. "They've been having these reunions for five years. No one has ever told me about them—either before or after. They could have told me when they were being planned. I could have been there, but they never even thought of me."

She looked at me quizzically. "I don't belong in that family. I just have never seemed to belong. Can you understand how I feel? They don't like me. I don't fit. I've never fit anywhere. I'm a stranger in this world. No one knows me or wants to know me, really. No one cares what I think or what I feel—or even if I think or feel. I have no one. I've never had anyone. I'm sick at the knowledge that I never will have anyone. Not in my whole life."

She was crying again, but quietly, almost with fatigue.

"I guess I can learn to talk to people and how to be friends. I can get so I can value what I'm doing in the world. I know I'm feeling better about myself as a person. But how do I deal with this feeling about my own family? This knowledge that they don't care if I live or die? It doesn't matter how nice, how wealthy, how smart, how kind or mean I am. They just don't care! Being loved and accepted by them is so important to me."

"Sylvia, do you think they're doing things to you, or ignoring you, to hurt you?"

"No," she said quickly. "I don't think I'm important enough to them for that. They just don't think of me at all. I can be right underfoot, and they won't remember to tell me what's going on.

"I remember when I was about 19 one of my brothers came home on leave from the army. He brought a friend with him. It was all very exciting to the whole family. He asked me if I would go out with his friend on a double date with him and his girl friend. I said sure. I fussed with myself all week to be ready and be dressed just right and everything. Ten minutes before we were supposed to be ready, they left the house and didn't come back for two hours. They never said a word to me about what was going on. When they came back it was like 'so what.' They watched TV and played checkers. I'd been in my room crying for two hours. I looked so awful I couldn't even come down stairs."

"They owed you an explanation."

"Well, I never got it. I felt ugly and unacceptable as a date. I think I still feel that way. Sometimes I think I can never heal if I can't find a way to forgive my family for not caring for me. When a man looks interested in me, I think he's going to find me as unacceptable as my brother did, and I start being afraid to be myself. I can't seem to forgive. I can't seem to forget, and I can't make myself trust anyone."

Waiting for her tears to stop, I prayed for her to be open to forgiving her family. I asked for the wisdom to help her into an understanding of them.

"Sylvia, I have to ask you again. Do you think your family knew the impact of what they were doing to you?"

"No," she said, shaking her head. "I don't think so. They do things to each other, and they don't even know it. They're careless of people's feelings—everyone's, not just mine. They don't know what they're doing. I'm convinced of that, although I think they should know what they're doing."

"I think Jesus knew some people like that, too."

"But He could avoid people that didn't believe in Him. And He had His apostles."

"Not always, Sylvia. He wasn't always able to avoid brutal, careless people. He didn't always have His apostles with Him either."

"What are you thinking of?"

"The crucifixion. Do you remember that the people of Jerusalem isolated Jesus and crucified Him with criminals? They totally ignored what He had done for them and what He had been to them. His apostles scattered to the winds when He needed their support the most. He was totally alone and misunderstood, abused and deprived. Yet He hung on that cross, and His prayer to His Father was, 'Forgive them, for they don't know what they are doing.'"

"I see," she said, rubbing her forehead. "I've got such a headache."

"I wish you could see that you share that moment of the Passion with Jesus in a very special way. I wish you would try to share Jesus' feelings when He prayed to His father for His persecutors. Ask Jesus to share your feelings. I wish you would try to do this. Try to love Jesus when you make this prayer."

"I'll try," she said gathering up her purse. "I'd try anything to change the way I feel inside about my family and about myself."

I wondered as I watched her leave what the Lord would say to her if she allowed herself to share His moment of forgiveness on the cross. I didn't have long to wait. Two hours later Sylvia called me.

"I hate to bother you," she said with a curious catch in her voice. "But I had to tell you what happened to me."

"You're no bother, Sylvia."

"I stopped at church on the way from your office. There was a noon Mass, so I attended. After Mass, I just sat in the pew and looked at Jesus on the cross. I tried to imagine how He felt, looking out at the people who had put Him there. I tried to feel the forgiveness He had to have felt for the world, but I couldn't. I tried to say I forgave my family, but I felt like a rock was cutting my throat in half. I felt like I couldn't breathe. So I tried to relax. Then I just tried to share the feelings of pain Jesus had at being misunderstood, ignored and abused. I could identify with those feelings, and I asked Him to let me share them. I tried to love Him and to feel my own feelings of rejection. It was really weird.

"What was weird?"

"What happened. It was like feeling so many things at once. I felt like someone was pouring ice water on my head only it wasn't cold. My thinking seemed to become very lucid in spite of the pain I was feeling. It was like I could understand fears and pain in my family that I hadn't been able to even recognize before. I felt a compassion for them and a consciousness that their blindness to the needs of myself and other people was a protection against their own pain."

"That is an insight. How are you feeling about them now?"

"Like they ought to face their pain instead of inflicting it on others. I feel tired of thinking about them but curiously separated from them. I feel untied. I don't know how to explain that exactly. It's just that I'm different and always have been. It doesn't mean there isn't some love there somewhere, but it's just not there in the way I need it. Yet I don't feel so devastated by the lack of their love right now."

"I'm glad you prayed with the Lord, Sylvia. It sounds like you've found a measure of peace."

"Actually a lot of peace," she laughed suddenly. "I'm glad I'm me, in spite of the pain. I'm glad my feelings weren't cut off so completely that I couldn't care about other people and their needs. I don't know how, but I'm going to make it. Someone, somewhere, is going to love me someday. I know it."

VIII

Jesus Again Before Pilate

Pilate then called together the chief priests, the ruling class, and the people, and said to them: "You have brought this man before me as one who subverts the people. I have examined him in your presence and have no charge against him arising from your allegations. Neither has Herod, who therefore has sent him back to us; obviously this man has done nothing that calls for death. Therefore I mean to release him, once I have taught him a lesson." The whole crowd cried out, "Away with this man; release Barabbas for us!" This Barabbas had been thrown in prison for causing an uprising in the city, and for murder. Pilate addressed them again, for he wanted Jesus to be the one he released.

But they shouted back, "Crucify him, crucify him!" He said to them for the third time, "What wrong is this man guilty of? I have not discovered anything about him that calls for the death penalty. I will therefore chastise him and release him." But they demanded with loud cries that he be crucified, and their shouts increased in violence. Pilate then decreed that what they demanded should be done. He released the one they asked for, who had been thrown in prison for insurrection and murder, and delivered Jesus up to their wishes.

Luke 23:13-25

"I'm really hurting." Bob shifted his weight in the chair and averted his eyes. "My whole life is in a shambles. My wife left me. Or rather locked me out of the house. Married 18 years and she said 'I don't want to be married to you anymore. Go away.'

"Just like that. Go away! Don't talk to me! And it's over. 18 years. I can't get her to talk to me about anything. The boys either. They're being very protective of their mother and won't have anything to do with me." He leaned back in his chair, his face twisted with grief. "I don't deserve this. I really don't. I took good care of my family."

He searched his pockets for a handkerchief and wiped his mouth nervously. "She's sued for divorce. She tied up our property. Even my retirement and insurance are involved. I'm essentially broke. I'm trying to fight, but I'm hurting so bad I can't think." He stopped and drew a deep breath. "Even my business is affected. I'm hanging on. But I'm sure my partners are moving to get rid of me. I can't deal with all this. I'm worn out, and I'm getting sick."

"When did she leave you, Bob?" I asked compassionately.

"Ten years ago. She sued me for divorce, but I've kept fighting it in court. It's not over. Not yet."

"Ten years!" I echoed. "Bob, you talk about it as if it were yesterday."

"It feels like yesterday. I can remember every word, every gesture, every second of every court date. I tried to reconcile over and over. I told her we were married. She couldn't divorce me. I wasn't willing. I told the judge he had no right to grant her a divorce, because it forced me into a divorce I didn't want. I told him he was taking away my rights. Sometimes I feel such a rage, I don't know how I control myself." His eyes blazed as he spoke, and he stopped speaking, his lips pressed together. His body squirmed with sudden tension.

We were both silent for a very long minute.

"Bob, the judge was right. No one should be forced to live with someone they don't want to live with."

"She took a vow to live with me! I honored my commitment. I was willing to spend my life with her. I didn't back out of my vow just because I wasn't always happy living with her."

"You weren't happy in the marriage?"

"She was my wife. I gave my word to love her and take care of her. I was doing that. I was keeping my end of our promise to each other. She backed out, and she still won't tell me what I did."

"After ten years, you're still trying to find out

what went wrong in your relationship?"

"I'd certainly like to know. I promised to protect her, to provide for her, to take care of the car, the yard," he gestured expansively. "I did that. I did what I was supposed to do, but she wasn't satisfied."

"But were you sharing with her? Talking, loving, growing through experiences together?"

"I was working," he stated with considerable energy. "I started a business and built it from the ground to provide for her and the boys like I was supposed to do. Now everything I worked for is being pulled out from under me. How am I supposed to feel?"

"What's happening in your business?"

"My partners are doing things without me. They've suggested I take a rest to try and get over Marie and the divorce. A couple of years ago they insisted on a psychiatric evaluation as part of our yearly physicals. I took all the tests and passed. They can't prove anything, but they're saying I'm paranoid. I don't think I am, but they want me out. I passed their doctor's tests. They can't prove anything, but they want to force me out. And they can . . . at the next stockholder's meeting.

"I'm literally fighting for survival. So far I've lost everything: my wife, my kids, my home, my savings, now my business. I can't take much more of this."

We sat quietly together, each of us lost in thought.

"No one will face me with what I'm doing wrong" he said finally, bitterly. "I'm doing everything I agreed to do, and I'm doing it well,

I think. But people gossip and slander me behind my back. I can't fight what I can only guess at."

"You don't know what you're doing wrong at the business?" I questioned gently.

"No, I don't know! They're not being up front with me. Just these innuendos and suggestions that I rest. I hate this situation!" He slammed his fist hard into his palm. "I'm losing everything, and all my life I've played it straight. I did what my parents, religious leaders, and teachers taught was right. But no one else does, and nobody else cares that I play it straight. Damn the authorities! I wish no one had ever taught me right from wrong."

"Right and wrong can be pretty relative, Bob," I ventured. "Life can get into some pretty sticky gray areas. That's where free will and an informed conscience take over."

"My free will would send me straight to hell," he thundered, his eyes blazing. "Are you sure you understand what I've been saying to you?"

"I think I do," I asserted with authority. "Ten years ago your wife and boys left you, and you question her right to do this. She sued for a share of the family assets, and you question the court's competence in granting her wishes, since you didn't want a divorce. You've lost family, property, money, and now your business partners are fighting you. You feel you've done nothing to deserve this, since you've maintained your role in each instance as defined by the church and the culture."

"That's right," he nodded.

"I hear you blaming the church, the culture, the

authorities for your present predicament."

"I do blame them," he drew himself erect in his chair and stared hard at me. "They taught me."

"By blaming them, you've denied your own responsibility in each of these situations."

"Responsibility!" he shouted. "I'm the most responsible person I know! If Marie had a shred of responsibility we'd still be married."

"She exercised her free will in a difficult situation. She's responsible for her behavior. You are responsible for yours."

"She's going to hell for breaking up a family and forcing me into adulterous affairs for a little comfort," he blurted out.

"She's responsible for her behavior, but she's not forcing you into any behavior. You are responsible for your own behavior. No one else is. As an adult you have a responsibility to develop an adult conscience for adult situations."

"I don't have any responsibility for my conscience. It was hammered into me as a kid, and I can't go against it today."

"What you were taught as a child was probably correct for a child's mind, but an adult's mind is different. You have an obligation to develop an adult informed conscience."

"As the twig is bent," he intoned majestically, "so grows the tree."

"I'll see you Friday," I answered stiffly.

He stood up. "How long is this going to take," he asked, suddenly submissive.

"A long time," I pronounced darkly.

* * * * *

I didn't expect to see him again, but he came without fail to every appointment. His grief and anger were devastating to him. It became apparent that he had entered marriage to have a home and the security of a family. He had not felt a special love for Marie and did not believe she had ever really loved him, even though she had said she had. What they did have was a verbal and legal commitment to each other, two sons, property and the security and closeness of family life. He acknowledged that he would have married any good Christian woman who was reasonably attractive. His feelings for his wife were largely possessive. His grief centered on his lost security within a family. This security was again threatened by the rupture of his relationship with his partners and the pending loss of his company. As the day of the stockholder's meeting drew closer, Bob's anxiety became acute.

"It's over," he announced one afternoon, sinking heavily into a chair. "My partners got enough proxies to swing the vote any way they want."

His fingers drummed nervously on the chair arm. "They stopped by my office with the company CPA who had a notarized count. They wanted to spare me the embarrassment of a public vote. I'm supposed to retire quietly," he spit out, "and stop being a problem to them."

He covered his face for a brief moment. "I'm glad it's over. I am sick. My gut feels like it's in pieces."

"In a way, it must be a relief," I agreed.

"But I still don't know what I did to make them so upset. Why should they treat me like this?

What have I done to them?"

"They've given you no idea?"

"Poor judgment. That's all I can get out of them. I hired those two twenty years ago! Poor judgment? I built that company with my own hands. It wasn't poor judgment then. I'm still the same businessman I was then. Dear God, I am sick." He buried his forehead in his hand. One tear, the only tear I had or would ever see from him, coursed down his cheek and fell to his shirt front.

I watched as the tear slowly darkened a spot where it fell—mute testimony to the internal agony raging within him.

"I am not wrong," he burst out. "I haven't done anything to deserve this treatment—and not from my wife either—or my boys. The whole world has turned on me. It has all my life. No one has ever been on my side. I can't trust anyone! I never have been able to!"

I started to speak, but he continued, shaking a finger at me.

"I am responsible. People know they can count on me. I do what I've been taught is fair. I follow the Commandments and the Bible exactly."

"I'm sure you do, Bob," I said. "I have no doubt that you follow the law exactly."

"So what have I done to deserve this?" he demanded. His eyes stared at me, confused and hurt.

I looked back at him thoughtfully. The same question. We'd talked so many times of his adherence to the biblical laws and roles taught to him in childhood while his relationships died from lack of nurturing. So many times we had covered this same question.

"Bob, that question comes out of the Passion of Jesus. Do you know that?"

His brow furrowed, thinking.

"Pilate asked the crowd that question about Jesus. What has he done? Why do you want to crucify him? What harm has this man done?"

Bob's eyes watched me cautiously, thoughtfully. He did not speak.

"Perhaps you share that moment of the Passion with Jesus, Bob. Maybe if you prayed about it, tried to unite your pain with the pain of Jesus, tried to share the feelings Jesus must have had when Pilate asked the crowd that question, 'What has he done?' and they only screamed, 'Crucify him!' People he had healed were there. People for whom he had shown compassion and love. These people were part of a crowd shouting to kill him. Perhaps Jesus could help you with that question, Bob, more than anyone else. He lived through that question, too."

Without a word, Bob stood up and walked to the door. He stopped there and looked back at me, his face a study in conflicting emotions, but his eyes were alive with a soft glow. He left, still silent.

* * * * *

"I'm sorry for the abrupt way I left at our last meeting," he apologized. "I had to leave, and I didn't dare talk."

My eyebrows raised in surprise. "Didn't *dare* talk?" I echoed.

"Something happened to me when you were talking about the Passion and Pilate saying, what has he done? It was like I was feeling something I had never felt before. I had to get away and be alone for a while."

"Felt something?" I questioned. "A feeling, Bob? What kind of feeling?"

"A fullness, a closeness. It was strange. I've never felt that kind of closeness to a single, living person, and I've wanted to. I imagined what it would be like to be really close to someone. This was more. I needed to be alone."

"I do understand."

We sat quietly together. He was more composed than I had ever seen him.

"I prayed and it was good," he said simply. "I felt close to God and kind of peaceful, but . . . " he hesitated, then shook his head and grimaced.

"I was aware I had never really pursued closeness with another person. I wanted it, but I was too busy being right to notice we weren't close.

"What has he done? Jesus didn't do anything to warrant that hatred. What have I done? Nothing. I haven't done anything either. I strangely felt peaceful and convicted at the same time. I'll never admit this again to anyone. But I had an impression of what you were trying to say about responsibility. It's a different kind of responsibility than I meant, but I was suddenly aware that I had never made my own choices. I didn't feel part of my own life. I have to learn how to make choices."

"And to be responsible for your own choices."

He nodded. "I've always done what I thought would be approved of by some authority."

"Then you could always blame the authority if things went wrong."

He shook a finger at me. "You're very good at finishing my sentences for me. Let's hope you're as good at teaching me to make good choices."

"Don't put that on me," I almost shouted, and we both laughed. "You jump in. You make your choices. You risk. You live with the mistakes, and you celebrate when, now and then, you do it right."

"I hope I can remember, when I don't want to risk, the way I feel right now."

"Go back to the Passion at those times," I advised him quickly. Know that the work you're doing on your self here each week is slow, but it is bearing fruit that will last in your personality."

IX

The Betrayal

After saying this, Jesus grew deeply troubled. He went on to give this testimony: "I tell you solemnly, one of you will betray me."

The disciples looked at one another, puzzled as to whom he could mean. One of them, the disciple whom Jesus loved, reclined close to him as they ate. Simon Peter signaled him to ask Jesus whom he meant. He leaned back against Jesus' chest and said to him, "Lord, who is he?" Jesus answered, "The one to whom I give the bit of food I dip in the dish." He dipped the morsel, then took it and gave it to Judas, son of Simon Iscariot. Immediately after, Satan entered his heart. Jesus addressed himself to him: "Be quick about what you are to do."

John 13:21-27

He had large blue eyes and a cocky smile. He would tell me many times in the days ahead how unhandsome he was. "But nobody, especially not women, cares because I'm so friendly. They don't even notice I'm short, too fat and balding. I can walk in a room and turn the whole place upside down in ten minutes—just by being friendly." Then he would demonstrate how he could smile as if he did not have a care in the world, as if the person he was with inspired a magic in him, as if he were filled with a mysterious energy that would never tire. "I'm the world's greatest salesman," he advised me without bravado. "That's just a fact. I can sell anything. Or anybody. I'm a million dollar salesman in every line of business I've been in. Companies fight over who will hire me. Nobody believes me, but it's true. I have job offers pending all the time. I can write my own ticket in any industry in this country and some out of the country."

"You appear to live a charmed life," I agreed with him on this first meeting. "What can I possibly do to improve on such a record?"

He leaned forward and stared at me intently. The smile faded and the light left his eyes. "I don't know if you can help me. I'm a mean, nasty, angry tyrant in my home. My soul rages with a hatred I don't begin to understand. I've been belligerent with my wife for 35 years, and she's always taken it. As a matter of fact she treated me better when I was mean than when I was acting decent."

"How did your kids respond to such treatment?" I asked.

"No kids," he waved his hand negatively. "No kids. I didn't want any kids slowing us down or getting between myself and Linda. I saw that in other marriages. All at once the wife has no time for the husband, just the kids. I didn't want that."

He glanced out the window. "Am I supposed to tell you everything? Yes, alright, well, Linda did get pregnant once. I told her not to, but she did. I had the baby placed upstate before Linda was back in her room. She never saw the baby, and she never got pregnant again. That's just fine with me."

"You left selfish off your list of personality defects," I observed, an anger for him beginning to touch my spirit.

"I know. I know. I'm a selfish, arrogant, driving hypocrite. I've heard it before. But you really don't understand. I've loved Linda since I was fifteen years old. I've never wanted anything except to be with her, to provide for her and to make her proud of me."

"By being mean to her? By giving her baby away?"

"She treated me better when I was mean to her. I told her if she ever got pregnant I'd get rid of the baby, and I told her why. I couldn't stand the thought of anyone between us. I couldn't."

"So you need help in your relationship with Linda?" I questioned.

"You could say that."

"Jim, I need you to be more specific about what you expect from therapy. I have the feeling there's something you're leaving out."

He got up and paced around the room, his hand

across his mouth. "I want to kill someone," he said finally. "I have this anger in me, and I can't live with it." He turned and looked directly at me. "She left me two weeks ago. I know Linda. She can't make it on her own. She's with someone. I know she is, and I'm going to kill him."

"How do you know she's with someone?"

"I've been following her. Following her every chance I get. I know where she's living. I've been there. I've pestered her till she let me in. I've talked with her, but she doesn't want to talk with me. She just wants me to walk away and never think about her again. I can't. I'm breaking in pieces. I don't know how to live without her. I don't care about business. I don't care about anything but getting her back."

"Will she come to therapy with you?"

"I don't think so, but it's worth a try. I don't think she'll do anything for me. It's like a curtain came down. I think she's been planning this for a long time. I don't think it was sudden with her."

"How do you know there's a man involved?"

"I've seen him. I've seen her go out with him. I've followed him home. I've followed her to his apartment. I know how to get to either of them."

"How serious are you about killing him?"

"I don't want to hurt anyone. I'm really a peaceful guy. I just want Linda. But this rage inside of me is awful. I question being able to control myself all of the time."

Linda did come to therapy. She came alone and described her life with Jim and her decision to leave him many years earlier.

"It took time to arrange things," she said calmly. "I had never worked. I had no money but his. I needed to get money saved to take care of myself. I had to learn how to earn a living for myself. I had to develop some friends that would support me when I left him. It took time. I haven't loved Jim for years."

"But why didn't you come to a therapist? With all the preparations you were making to leave him, why didn't you try to work out the problems while you still loved him. He doesn't want to lose you."

"He wouldn't have come to therapy."

"He's here now. He would have come if you'd been firm about it."

"While I loved him, I couldn't be firm with him. I was too afraid of losing him. I fell in love with Jim when I was a kid. I would have done anything he asked. There were things I didn't like about him. But he never heard me when I mentioned to him that I wished he'd change. He just didn't hear. I lived his way as long as I could. I just can't face the rest of my life with someone that can't hear me, that never can accommodate or understand that I have needs too."

"What about the baby?"

"He told you about the baby? My, is he ever being honest these days! We've never talked about the baby. He said 'OK' when he first learned I was pregnant, but then he said I was too happy pregnant."

"Too happy?"

"I loved everything about being pregnant. I loved the changes in my body. I loved the feeling of the baby when it began to move. I even loved being tired. I can still remember it. I guess I became very involved with myself—with my feelings, and my needs and the changes going on inside of me. I know I became kind of emotional at times. He just couldn't understand and felt the baby would come between us. He felt deprived. He said he couldn't feel anything for the baby. It wasn't real to him. I was real to him. He was real to him. But the baby was not real to him. I never saw the baby. I don't even know if it was a boy or girl. I couldn't find out either. No one would tell me. Perhaps it was best that way. It was like it died or had never been." She was silent, her lower lip pulled so tight that her chin changed its shape. Then the tears began to fall.

"I forgave him. At least I tried to. I tried to understand the kind of love he had for me that could not even extend to a baby. It seemed to spoil the pregnancy for me those last months. I became so fearful of losing the baby that I had to accept the inevitable or lose my mind. That's the choice I found myself in. Losing my baby or my mind."

"Or your husband?"

"I couldn't even consider losing Jim at that time. That was thirty years ago. I loved him and believed in him."

Linda continued to love him until, as she expressed it, he began keeping secrets from her. As the years went by she found him staying away from home, not including her in business trips as he had done in the early years of their marriage, exploding with rage at her about his business affairs but not sharing the concerns that he felt. He left her alone once too often, for several days. She had given her life careful thought during those days and had decided to prepare to leave him. When the time was right for her, she left. She had no intention of returning. Jim was not prepared.

Linda agreed to meet with Jim in therapy a few times to help him adjust to the inevitable. She was so completely unmoved by his charm, his logic and his entreaties that he began to reach an understanding that the relationship was, indeed, ended.

Somewhere during the course of his efforts at reconciliation, Jim returned to the church of his youth. He confided in me that he had not been to church since his wedding but that he had found himself turning to God in his loneliness and pain.

"I'm hoping God can help me," he said one afternoon. "I'm praying a lot, but this is really tearing me up. I can't adjust to her being gone. I don't want her with anyone else. My insides just burn at the thought. I feel such anger and betrayal. I saw her going out the other night. She looked so good."

"Jim, are you still following her around?"

"I may never stop," he answered seriously. "I can't let go of her. I just want to look at her. It's tearing me to pieces."

"You have to stop following her around. You have to stop spying on her. She's made a clean break. Let her go. Work on yourself. Work out why you needed such a possessive love. Let her go."

"I can't. I try. God knows I've tried." He pounded the arm of the chair hard for a minute. "Do you realize how she betrayed me? Those last years she pretended to love me. For years she let me say things to her, make love to her. Yet she was planning to leave me all that time. She's got to come back to me. I can't stand the betrayal."

"She's not coming back, Jim."

"Don't say that!"

"It has to be said. You've had your chance to convince her of your good intentions toward her, of your love for her. She is not coming back."

"I can't live without her."

"You can. You have been for several months now. You're going to find someone else to love, and you'll be a more considerate husband this time."

"I can't stand the pain. I can't stand the pain. Why can't you understand that I can't stand the pain. It's not getting any better. I can stand the thought of her leaving me if that will make her happy. I really want her happy. What I can't stand is the idea of the betrayal. God, that hurts! I have to live with that for the rest of my life! She lived with me for years planning to leave me. With other people knowing what she was doing. It hurts! She just cut me off like a stranger—after 35 years!"

"His body writhed in tension. He jumped to his feet and paced about the room, his face grimacing with pain.

"Sometimes I feel," he said, dropping back into the chair, "that there is no way to relieve this pain without killing someone."

"A few minutes ago you were saying that you hoped God could help you. Perhaps that is the best way for you to go, Jim. I have found that, being realistic about life and emotions and the hurts that we encounter in living, there are some situations and some pains that we have to learn to bear somehow. Perhaps this pain of betrayal is a pain you have to learn to tolerate and to live with."

"How? Just tell me how? That's all I'm asking for!"

"In the Passion of Christ, Jim, Jesus is betrayed by someone who has lived with him for years."

"Peter?"

"I was thinking of Judas. At the last supper, Jesus turned to him and said, 'What you have to do, do quickly.' Do you remember that Judas never returned, never forgave or asked to be forgiven for his betrayal?"

"Don't say those words! They torture me," his face grimaced again. His neck twisted his head around to the side in an uncontrollable spasm.

"Try to share Jesus' feelings of that moment, Jim. Try to feel what Jesus was feeling about the love he had shown Judas, and the rejection and the betrayal he was receiving. Try to share your feelings with Jesus. Try to love Jesus while you're sharing."

"I'll try," he said jumping to his feet. "I'll try on my way home. I'll try immediately."

Jim was in an angry mood when he arrived for his next appointment. He had been following Linda again and he had, again, seen her with another man. He had also found a girlfriend who seemed to be willing to take the time to listen to his pain. As he recited the events of the past week and the feelings he had experienced seeing Linda that morning, I noted a new degree of control about his speech and body movements. He stopped talking suddenly and stared at me, as if in surprise.

"That prayer you suggested for me. Do you know what happened?"

"No," I answered. "Tell me."

"It doesn't work driving. I couldn't do it while I was doing anything else. I have to really concentrate on just that prayer. It's really something. The pain stops. The pain stops completely during that prayer. I get freedom from the pain and a feeling of peace. The pain comes back after a while. Everytime I stop and do that prayer, the pain leaves. But it takes real effort."

"That's great. I'm really glad you found a way to ease your pain."

"I am too," he said thoughtfully. "I can control the pain with that prayer. I'll probably still do dumb things for a while—like following Linda and blaming her for what she did—but I know I can stop the pain.

"I know there are a lot of things I have to work out about myself. But now I've got some space to work on myself. I was really afraid, sometimes, when I'd feel that pain, that I was going to hurt someone before I could figure myself out. Now I know I can work on my divorce from Linda, and I can stop the pain when I need to. I feel close to God. I feel protected. And that's real freedom."

X

The Agony in the Garden

Then he went out and made his way, as was his custom, to the Mount of Olives; his disciples accompanied him. On reaching the place he said to them, "Pray that you may not be put to the test." He withdrew from them about a stone's throw, then went down on his knees and prayed in these words: "Father, if it is your will, take this cup from me; yet not my will but yours be done." An angel then appeared to him from heaven to strengthen him.

Luke 22:39-43

"We've been married a week," she said, her eyes bright. "I think we've made a mistake. I want out."

"A week!" I exclaimed. "How can you know you've made a mistake in a week? How long did you know each other before you were married?"

"A year," he said quickly. We've been living together for the last six months. I don't know what happened, but she got strange the minute we got back from our honeymoon."

I looked back at her and raised an eyebrow. "What happened?"

"His feet stink," she said and giggled. "He wears tacky clothes to work, and he won't take a bath every day."

"You didn't know those things before you got married? You've been living together for six months and you didn't know he had stinky feet? Let's get serious!"

We sat and stared at each other curiously. She was tall and pretty with eyes that promised mischief. I looked back at her husband of one week. He was also tall, unusually handsome and with an air of dignified, suffering impatience.

"My feet do stink," he admitted, a little sheepishly.

"Everybody's feet stink," I exclaimed.

"Well, mine can get pretty rank. I have to admit that. But I do try to keep them clean. I wear open weave shoes so the air can get to them and keep them dry. I am trying."

"What do you think is going on?" I asked him.

"It's like I said. I don't know. She's moved out of the bedroom, and she's getting ready to move back to her mother's. I'm having a hard time believing all this."

"Cindy, perhaps we'd better talk alone for a while."

"No. I can talk in front of Lee." she straightened

in her chair. "It's just that I don't know how to say it."

"Straight out." I advised her. "Any words that come close. We can try to refine it after."

"He's gotten mean."

"Mean!" he exclaimed. "I have not. I've not laid a hand on her."

"You have too," she contradicted loudly.

"I don't believe this," he shouted, his face a tangle of emotions. He ran his hand through his hair and held it there, took a deep breath and stared at the ceiling. "I don't believe this. I have not laid a hand on her in anger."

"I didn't say you hit me. I said you've gotten mean. And you have. You're nagging me all the time. You've criticized everything I've done for the last two weeks. I don't like it."

"Criticize. Nag. That's not mean."

"I told you I didn't know how to say what I meant. But it's mean to me. I don't want to live like that."

"Wait," I said, "let's let each other talk. Don't just jump on each other. Hear each other out. Give the other person a chance to explain what he's trying to say. Something happened to you two weeks ago., What was it?"

"I was trying to get ready for a wedding. I don't know what I did," she said, starting to cry. "He was no help."

"Cindy, I wish you wouldn't do that. It makes me feel awful."

"Lee, what happened two weeks ago?"

"I don't know," he rested his head against the

97

back of the couch and looked at the ceiling. "I guess I just got scared."

"Of what?"

"Scared of being married. Scared of trying to cope with Cindy. She can be so temperamental at times. When we moved in together, she was working. She's an LVN. It was supposed to be for kicks. I didn't really bargain on falling in love with her, but I did. I really did. We talked about babies, and she agreed to no babies."

"You're pregnant?" I asked her. She nodded.

"She agreed to no babies," he said again. "All at once we're having a baby. I feel like I'm a little young for the responsibility of a baby, but it is my baby so we decided to get married." He stopped and looked at her. Their eyes caught and after a moment she looked at me.

"I didn't mean to get pregnant. It just happened. You'd think it was all my fault. Yes, I want a baby more than he does, but I didn't do this on purpose."

"It's not the baby so much," he spoke up quickly. "I don't feel like a father. I don't feel like I'm ready for the responsibility of a baby, but it's mine. I'll do my best to take care of it and her. But we have no money saved. The bank account is zero. We're in a rented apartment with rented furniture, in an adult building. We'll have to move when the baby comes."

"That's a bad spot to be in."

"A week before the wedding I learned from her brother that she had quit her job."

"I didn't quit my job!" she bridled. "I gave my notice for a month before the baby is due."

"The notice was for a quit, not a pregnancy leave. I've just been upset. I think she should have talked with me about it. I think we should be making decisions together. I think she should keep on working. We're in this together. If she leaves me, she'll have to work. Why can't she work and live with me?"

"Because you've gotten mean," she stated emphatically.

"You'd stay with him if he wasn't so critical of you?" I asked.

"Well, I loved him. That's why I married him. I wouldn't have married him, even if I were pregnant, if I didn't love him. I want this to work, but I don't want to be abused."

"I think," I said quietly, "that you two need training in communication skills. The baby isn't due for several months, so you'll both be working for a while. There is no need for an immediate decision. Suppose that we work on building some lines of communication between you and worry about the divorce later."

Lee and Cindy agreed to my suggestion. They started working on learning about each other and how to communicate effectively. It was an uphill battle in many ways. They were young and stubborn about their rights. Both came from homes where both parents were not present. They had become involved with each other physically long before they had known the personality and emotional needs of the other.

In their efforts to please the other and to maintain the relationship, they had ignored their own needs assuming that love would somehow magically clear the problems away. As they got to know each other, they found many areas of immaturity in themselves and in each other. Both had a tendency for humor which bordered on heavy sarcasm.

Although their relationship improved, it was still far from perfect when the baby was born.

"It's D-Day," Lee said to me as we stood outside the nursery looking at his new son. "I don't know what to do. I love her more than ever, but I don't know if we'll ever grow up enough to be good for each other or for him."

"You're both so strong-willed," I agreed, "but you're both trying. That's terribly important. How is she feeling about staying with you now that the baby is here?"

"No different than when we saw you last week," he shrugged. "We've talked to our minister who is appalled with us. We've prayed about it. I think I'm still scared. I just don't feel ready for the responsibility of a wife and a kid. I don't know how to get out of this without hurting everyone including myself."

"Maybe you really need to take this to the Lord in a special way."

"I've prayed," he said morosely.

"Lee, maybe you need to realize that the Lord was faced with a task He didn't feel ready to deal with either. He prayed for his father to take it away."

"Let this cup pass me by."

"Right. Lee, I've found that people are given some powerful answers to their prayers when they can share a moment of the Passion with

Jesus. I think each of us has a moment of the Passion in our lives. Perhaps this is your moment. Perhaps making this decision to stay with Cindy or to leave is your moment of the Passion to share with Jesus."

"How do you share something like that?" he asked.

"Ask the Holy Spirit to guide you. Then think of the Lord and how He must have been feeling. Try to feel what he was going through and love Him. Ask Him to share your burden of decision and ask Him to let you share His burden of decision. He'll help you. I know He will. It isn't an easy prayer. You really have to put your heart into it."

He looked down at me wearily. "I don't know if I have enough heart for anything," he said. "I feel so deprived. I can't even buy a pair of socks or go to a movie or buy a beer without feeling guilty about the money, and now I've got a baby. I'm 22 years old and I feel 50. But I'll try. I'll tell Cindy about it. We'll both give your prayer a shot."

* * * * *

When they came to my office the following week, I was pleased to see that they appeared to be sharing the responsibilities of carrying the baby and its belongings.

"How is everything going?" I asked, as they gave me the baby to hold. "He is beautiful. He looks so alert and happy."

"We're OK," Cindy stated tersely. "We decided

to give it a try together. It's going to be awfully hard. We just never knew how much we didn't know about each other. But we prayed like you said, and we haven't really felt like separating."

Lee nodded. "We came away from that prayer with a strange kind of peace. I guess we both felt somehow strengthened personally and tolerant of each other. I know we need to work on our attitudes a lot, but praying together has really helped. With both of us praying this sharing prayer, we know where we both are about each other. If that makes any kind of sense."

"Sure it makes sense," I nodded.

"That prayer is different," Cindy remarked. "We both felt really anointed that first time we did it."

"Anointed?" I questioned.

"It was at the hospital. I was telling Cindy about it. The nurse brought Timmy in for feeding, so we held Timmy and each other, and we tried to share that moment with Jesus together. We felt so close to each other. I can't begin to describe it. We've had some disputes since, but I can't seem to feel any real anger toward Cindy."

"It's been really good," Cindy added. "It's like God has become part of our decision to be together and part of our relationship together. I feel like we have a strength we didn't have before."

"Praise God." I said quietly.

XI

The Way of the Cross

Jesus, however, he first had scourged; then he handed him over to be crucified. The procurator's soldier took Jesus inside the praetorium and collected the whole cohort around him. They stripped off his clothes and wrapped him in a scarlet military cloak. Weaving a crown out of thorns they fixed it on his head, and stuck a reed in his right hand. Then they began to mock him by dropping to their knees before him, saying, "All hail, king of the Jews!" They also spat at him. Afterward they took hold of the reed and kept striking him on the head. Finally, when they had finished making a fool of him, they stripped him of the cloak, dressed him in his own clothes, and led him off to crucifixion.

On their way out they met a Cyrenian named Simon. This man they pressed into service to carry the cross. Upon arriving at a site called Golgotha (a name which means Skull Place), they gave him a drink of wine flavored with gall, which he tasted but refused to drink.

When they had crucified him, they divided his clothes among them by casting lots; then they sat down there and kept watch over him.

Matthew 27:26-36

Who would believe what we have heard?
To whom has the arm of the Lord been revealed?
He grew up like a sapling before him, like a shoot from the parched earth;
There was in him no stately bearing to make us look at him,
Nor appearance that would attract us to him.
He was spurned and avoided by men, a man of suffering, accustomed to infirmity,
One of those from whom men hide their faces,
Spurned, and we held him in no esteem.
Yet it was our infirmities that he bore,
Our sufferings that he endured,
While we thought of him as stricken,
As one smitten by God and afflicted.
But he was pierced for our offenses, crushed for our sins;
Upon him was the chastisement that makes us whole,
By his stripes we were healed.
We had all gone astray like sheep, each following his own way;
But the Lord laid upon him the guilt of us all.
Though he was harshly treated, he submitted
And opened not his mouth;
Like a lamb led to the slaughter or a sheep before the shearers,
He was silent and opened not his mouth.

Oppressed and condemned, he was taken
  away,
And who would have thought any more of his
  destiny?
When he was cut off from the land of the
  living,
and smitten for the sin of his people,
A grave was assigned him among the wicked
And a burial place with evildoers,
Though he had done no wrong nor spoken any
  falsehood.
But the Lord was pleased to crush him in
  infirmity.
If he gives his life as an offering for sin,
He shall see his descendants in a long life,
And the will of the Lord shall be accomplished
  through him.
Because of his affliction he shall see the light
  in fullness of days;
Through his suffering, my servant shall justify
  many, and their guilt he shall bear.
Therefore I will give him his portion among
  the great,
And he shall divide the spoils with the mighty,
Because he surrendered himself to death and
  was counted among the wicked;
And he shall take away the sins of many, and
  win pardon for their offenses.

           Isaiah 53:1-12

Additional books from
LIVING FLAME PRESS
Available at your bookstore or from
Living Flame Press, Locust Valley, N.Y. 11560

SPIRITUAL DIRECTION
Contemporary Readings   5.95

Edited by Kevin Culligan, O.C.D. The revitalized ministry of spiritual direction is one of the surest signs of renewal in today's Church. In this book seventeen leading writers and spiritual directors discuss history, meaning, demands and practice of this ministry. Readers of the book should include not just a spiritual elite, but the entire Church — men and women, clergy and laity, members of religious communities.

PRAYER:
The Eastern Tradition   2.95

Andrew Ryder, S.C.J. In the East there is no sharp distinction between prayer and theology. Far from being divorced they are seen as supporting and completing each other. One is impossible without the other. Theology is not an end in itself, but rather a means, a way to union with God.

THE RETURNING SUN
Hope for a Broken World   2.50

George A. Maloney, S.J. In this collection of meditations, the author draws on his own experiences rooted in Eastern Christianity to aid the reader to enter into the world of the "heart." It is hoped that through contemplation of this material he/she will discover the return of the inextinguishable Sun of the universe, Jesus Christ, in a new and more experiential way.

BREAD FOR THE EATING   2.95

Kelly B. Kelly. Sequel to the popular *Grains of Wheat*, this small book of words received in prayer draws the reader closer to God through the imagery of wheat being processed into bread. The author shares her love of the natural world.

LIVING HERE AND HEREAFTER
Christian Dying,
Death and Resurrection 2.95

Msgr. David E. Rosage. The author offers great comfort to us by dispelling our fears and anxieties about our life after this earthly sojourn. Based on God's Word as presented in Sacred Scripture, these brief daily meditations help us understand more clearly and deeply the meaning of suffering and death.

PRAYING WITH SCRIPTURE
IN THE HOLY LAND
Daily Meditations With the Risen Jesus 3.50

Msgr. David E. Rosage. Herein is offered a daily meeting with the Risen Jesus in those Holy Places which He sanctified by His human presence. Three hundred and sixty-five scripture texts are selected and blended with the pilgrimage experiences of the author, a retreat master, and well-known writer on prayer.

DISCERNMENT:
Seeking God in Every Situation 3.50

Rev. Chris Aridas. "Many Christians struggle with ways to seek, know and understand God's plan for their lives. This book is prayerful, refreshing and very practical for daily application. It is one to be read and used regularly, not just read" *(Ray Roh, O.S.B.).*

DISCOVERING
PATHWAYS TO PRAYER .2.95

Msgr. David E. Rosage. Following Jesus was never meant to be dull, or worse, just duty-filled. Those who would aspire to a life of prayer and those who have already begun, will find this book amazingly thorough in its scripture-punctuated approach.

"A simple but profound book which explains the many ways and forms of prayer by which the person hungering for closer union with God may find him" *(Emmanuel Spillane, O.C.S.O., Abbot, Our Lady of the Holy Trinity Abbey, Huntsville, Utah).*

MOURNING: THE HEALING JOURNEY 2.95

Rev. Kenneth J. Zanca. Comfort for those who have lost a loved one. Out of the grief suffered in the loss of both parents within two months, this young priest has written a sensitive, sympathetic yet humanly constructive book to help others who have lost loved ones. This is a book that might be given to the newly bereaved.

THE BORN-AGAIN CATHOLIC 3.95

Albert H. Boudreau. This book presents an authoritative imprimatur treatment of today's most interesting religious issue. The author, a Catholic layman, looks at Church tradition past and present and shows that the born-again experience is not only valid, but actually is Catholic Christianity at its best. The exciting experience is not only investigated, but the reader is guided into revitalizing his or her own Christian experience. The informal style, colorful personal experiences, and helpful diagrams make this book enjoyable and profitable reading.

WISDOM INSTRUCTS HER CHILDREN
The Power of the Spirit and the Word 3.50

John Randall, S.T.D. The author believes that now is God's time for "wisdom." Through the Holy Spirit, "power" has become much more accessible in the Church. Wisdom, however, lags behind and the result is imbalance and disarray. The Spirit is now seeking to pour forth a wisdom we never dreamed possible. This outpouring could lead us into a new age of Jesus Christ! This is a badly needed, most important book, not only for the Charismatic Renewal, but for the whole Church.

GRAINS OF WHEAT 2.95

Kelly B. Kelly. This little book of words received in prayer is filled with simple yet often profound leadings, exhortations and encouragement for daily living. Within the pages are insights to help one function as a Christian, day by day, minute by minute.

LIVING FLAME PRESS
Box 74, Locust Valley, N.Y. 11560

QUANTITY

- _____ Journey Into Contemplation—3.95
- _____ Spiritual Direction—5.95
- _____ The Returning Sun—2.50
- _____ Prayer: the Eastern Tradition—2.95
- _____ Living Here and Hereafter—2.95
- _____ Praying With Scripture in the Holy Land—3.50
- _____ Discernment—3.50
- _____ Mourning: The Healing Journey—2.95
- _____ The Born-Again Catholic—3.95
- _____ Wisdom Instructs Her Children—3.50
- _____ Discovering Pathways to Prayer—2.95
- _____ Grains of Wheat—2.95
- _____ Bread for the Eating—2.95

NAME_____

ADDRESS _____

CITY_____ STATE_____ ZIP_____

Kindly include $.70 postage and handling on orders up to $5; $1.00 on orders up to $10; more than $10 but less than $50, add 10% of total; over $50, add 8% of total. Canadian residents add 20% exchange rate, plus postage and handling. N.Y. State residents add 7% tax unless exempt.